"They're "Rugby Boys"….Don't You Know?"

by

Natalie Vellacott

2nd Edition, published in 2014 by **Natalie Vellacott**

Text Copyright © Natalie Vellacott 2014

Illustrations and cover design Copyright © Lauren Densham 2014

Maps Copyright © Google 2014

Edited by Jenny Oberst

This account is a true story. Names of the street boys have been changed to protect their identities but all other names remain the same.

This book is not for profit and all royalties will be paid directly to "Olongapo Christian Help and Hope" for the ongoing support of the ministry.

ISBN 978 1502994929

Contents

Port Schedule of Logos Hope During my Time On-Board

September 2011 - September 2013

Colombo, Sri Lanka	Aug 29th, 2013	Sep 23rd, 2013
Phuket, Thailand	Aug 14th, 2013	Aug 24th, 2013
Singapore, Singapore	Aug 11th, 2013	Aug 11th, 2013
Kuching, Malaysia	Jul 11th, 2013	Aug 9th, 2013
Puerto Princesa, Philippines	Jul 2nd, 2013	Jul 8th, 2013
Subic Bay, Philippines	Jun 11th, 2013	Jul 1st, 2013
San Fernando, Philippines	May 24th, 2013	Jun 10th, 2013
Hong Kong, SAR China	Mar 20th, 2013	May 21st, 2013
Bangkok, Thailand	Feb 20th, 2013	Mar 13th, 2013
Sihanoukville, Cambodia	Feb 3rd, 2013	Feb 19th, 2013
Hong Kong, SAR China	Dec 15th, 2012	Jan 29th, 2013
Subic Bay, Philippines	Mar 16th, 2012	Dec 12th, 2012
Manila, Philippines	Feb 16th, 2012	Mar 15th, 2012
Cebu, Philippines	Jan 10th, 2012	Feb 14th, 2012
Singapore, Singapore	Dec 16th, 2011	Jan 4th, 2012
Kota Kinabalu, Malaysia	Nov 17th, 2011	Dec 13th, 2011
Kuching, Malaysia	Oct 27th, 2011	Nov 15th, 2011
Port Klang, Malaysia	Sep 28th, 2011	Oct 24th, 2011
Penang, Malaysia	Aug 18th, 2011	Sep 27th, 2011

Introduction

In late September 2011, I and approximately seventy-five others walked excitedly up the gangway of the Logos Hope Christian Missionary ship for the first time. The ship was in Penang, Malaysia having just begun its' tour of South East Asia. Prior to my enquiries in relation to this commitment, I had not heard of the ship and had never been to Asia. I was also ignorant of a large group of Islands in this region known as the Philippines. My English friends would not be that surprised by this as, until relatively recently, I wasn't sure where Wales was and had confused Lakeside with the Lake District.

On making this journey into the unknown, I knew only that the ship was said to be the largest floating Book Fair in the world and that it was to be my home for the next two years. I was to live and work on-board with four hundred fellow born-again Christians from a total of approximately sixty-five nationalities. The saving grace, for me anyway, was that the common spoken language on-board was to be English. I learned that this ship would travel from port to port, remaining for about three weeks in each, and then from country to country to bring knowledge, help and hope to the residents of each place. The floating Book Fair, being the largest in the world, brings knowledge with a wide selection of reasonably priced books including Christian, Educational, Hobbies, Cookery, Novels and anything else you can think of. The crew members bring help through practical work, medical and dental missions, donations of food and other items, and in other ways. Every crew member has a story of how Jesus has changed their life personally and they seek to share this with both the visitors to the Book Fair and people they meet on-shore, bringing hope to all nations of the world. From the outset it was the "hope" part that I was most interested in.

This story really begins on March 12th 2012 when the Logos Hope sailed into a lesser known part of the world called Subic Bay in the Philippines. This was just another port in one of many countries. The only planned difference was that the ship was due for its mandatory annual servicing and maintenance whilst stationed in this port and some major repairs were required. Still, the scheduled time in the dry dock was just a little over two months which seemed reasonable. For the work to be carried out and the ship to be properly inspected it had to be partially lifted out of the water hence the term "dry dock."

Many things happened after this date to keep the ship there in Subic Bay far beyond its intended stay, and even when it did eventually break free and sail on to new pastures it wasn't long before it would be back. It seems there was a driving force underneath and around the waters of the ship leading, guiding and directing its path to this place time and time again.

The Bible says in Proverbs 16 vs 9 "In their hearts humans plan their course, but the Lord establishes their steps." (NIV)

This was definitely true for the people making the decisions on Logos Hope and I was soon to be drastically changed as here, in Subic Bay, I encountered a group of street teenage boys known in the Philippines as "the rugby boys."

1: The Bridge

Whenever I mention "the bridge" people assume I am speaking about the control centre of the Logos Hope Ship. This is probably the most reasonable and logical assumption, being that at the time of most of the discussions, I was living on-board the said ship. Actually the bridge I am referring to has nothing whatsoever to do with the ship and is just a normal bridge about one hundred metres long and ten metres wide, made of concrete and about a twenty-five minute walk from the ship's berth at Rivera Wharf, Subic Bay Freeport Zone (SBFZ.) It is separated into three partitions by railings and the middle partition is covered.

The bridge allows most people to cross the dirty, polluted, and non-flowing Kalaklan river situated between SBFZ and Olongapo City (pronounced O-lon-gap-oh, not Apongalo or Opangola or any of the other English variations I have heard that bear little or no resemblance to how it reads, let alone how it sounds!) I say most people because there are numerous guards at a specially placed guard station at the SBFZ end of the bridge 24/7. Having said that, I never saw them stop anyone from crossing, with the exception of the "rugby boys" that is, but then in the minds of the security officers and many local people, they don't count.

Fortunately, at the point that I was dying of boredom on the ship (as it was seemingly caught in some sort of time capsule, unable to conclude its dry dock repairs), some crew members used their initiative and went hunting for a suitable location to carry out some weekend street evangelism. They chose the bridge to set up a book table as it was an ideal location due to the quantity of people traffic flowing across it on a regular basis. It would also provide shelter from the rain as we entered the rainy season. On hearing of this project, I stopped whinging to Dan (the Personnel Manager on the ship) that I was bored and didn't have anything to do and hightailed it down to the bridge every Saturday to be involved in the new ministry which combined two of my passions: Evangelism and Literature.

Our book table stocked the cheapest Christian books and local language Bibles from the Book Fair. We were authorised to give Bibles away for free if we had a good conversation or if someone really wanted one and couldn't afford it. Our primary goal was to engage people in conversation about Christianity, to share the Gospel with them and to offer to pray with them. We gained their attention by singing Christian songs and later through some preaching.

On the first Saturday (7th July 2012) there were at least ten crew members involved, but after this the interest waned, as it often does with street evangelism. There was still a regular group of four or five of us that continued the ministry. Initially the permission was just for Saturdays, but this was later revised to six days a week.

As we were now going to the bridge daily, we started to get to know the people that lived and worked in the vicinity. Our new friends included a blind man with a really great voice, that sometimes sang Christian songs and a lady that had been selling home cooked food on the bridge for over 30 years!

We obtained permission from a local church to use their facilities to store our books and other items each day after an initial attempt to lug everything back and forth from the ship was abandoned. This was a handy arrangement although one day when I asked a lady from the church if they had any "chairs" she disappeared to the store room for a while returning after ten minutes with a "chess" set and handed it to me announcing "chess." The funny thing was that it hadn't seemed a somewhat bizarre request for me to make of her in the first place, as she had gone straight away to find it!

Soon after starting the ministry, I saw a large group of boys congregating in an area underneath and to the side of the bridge several times a day and sometimes remaining there for long periods of time. They were doing something in their group but I couldn't see what it was as we were about fifty metres away. The boys were underneath a covered concrete area that ran at a ninety degree angle to the bridge leading away from it. From my vantage point, on the bridge, I had a good view of their comings and goings although I couldn't see the detail of their activity. Sometimes the younger boys stood naked in a circle and there was a lot of shouting and noise from the area. They looked like they were aged ten to twenty years old and there were about twenty of them in the group.

Not long after our arrival, some of the younger boys came to check us out. To do this they had to scramble out from their place of residence, along a pipe balanced precariously against a large wall, and then climb up and through a hole in a piece of board at the top of a fence. Then they could either walk around and join the common people in the covered walkway or use their preferred option, entering the restricted area running parallel to the covered area with just a wire fence separating the two partitions. The boys approached us from the other side of the fence in various stages of undress asking our names, ages, countries and what we were doing. We told them who we were and asked them some similar questions.

I put my hand through the fence towards them and they immediately grabbed it as if it was fascinating, started looking at it and then began gently stroking my fingers. I wondered what on earth they were doing and then they started softly saying "white white." They were talking about the flecks of white under my finger nails. I knew that this was a novelty for them as they weren't used to seeing white people and that they weren't going to do anything too drastic. Later in our ministry the boys were stroking the legs of a white crew member in a similar fashion but he asked them to stop as he was afraid the locals might think he had paid them to do it. I thought this was a bit unlikely but he said "Well, some people like some weird things!"

After a while the boys said "swimming, swimming." Then they moved away from the fence, stripped off the remainder of their clothes and climbed up the barriers on the edge of the bridge, which had obviously been erected to prevent people falling into the river. Many local people stopped to watch this spectacle and to take pictures. One by one the boys launched themselves into the filthy and shallow water less than ten metres below, shouting things to each other before climbing back up to repeat the process many times. The local people, although keen to watch, pulled faces of disgust or annoyance and made comments reflecting their obvious distaste. Some of the taller boys hit the floor of the river when they jumped in as mud came up with them when they surfaced. They didn't seem concerned about this but just laughed and continued shouting to each other. They seemed really joyful and happy, having a great time.

The security officers, obviously under pressure from the local people to do "something" about this lack of propriety in their city, headed down to engage the boys in conversation. However, the boys were not keen on being engaged and took off across the river swimming frantically and using various pieces of wood as floats and rafts. The officers, on seeing that they were fighting a losing battle and not really seeming to know what they would say to the boys in any event, soon gave up and slipped away. Seeing that they were safe again, the boys came back to the river bank, got out of the water, got dressed, and disappeared under the bridge. Interestingly, when the boys were being chased, I found myself rooting for them and hoping they would make good their escape, not siding with the officials as I might have expected myself to. I could see that the officials were not acting out of care or concern for the boys and that their only intention was to punish them for their bad behaviour. This was my first experience of the "rugby boys."

2 : "Rugby Boys"

At various points over the next few days I could see the boys in their hideout again, so I tried to work out what they were doing. They seemed to be holding plastic bags with something inside, which they were placing over their nose and inhaling from. This process was being repeated several times before the bags were placed into pockets for later or passed around amongst the group. Some of the boys were fighting imaginary characters further along the river bank, away from the bigger group. They were drawing swords and crouching in fighting positions, then engaging in combat with the air. I realised that the bags must contain some type of substance that was making them hallucinate. This realisation brought sadness and disbelief as some of the boys were really young and no doubt unaware of the dangers of solvent abuse.

The shocking thing was that, as mentioned already, there were police and security around at all times, due to the nearby guard station, but none of them were doing anything about this. The boys seemed invisible to them. Sometimes they watched them as if they couldn't do anything about it or as if they weren't really seeing them. On a few occasions, after I realised that the children were inhaling solvents, I asked the guards to intervene. However, they didn't seem to know what to do and just made comments like "they are there every day" and "rugby boys" and "not from our province so no jurisdiction." I was pretty frustrated by their inadequacy and lack of real concern.

On returning to the ship that evening, I carried out some research (on Wikipedia,) into this substance which I had been told was household glue called "rugby." I was really upset by my findings. The problem of these "rugby boys" had appeared everywhere in the Philippines and other third world countries. Children as young as 5 and 6 use it to stave off the hunger pangs that they get due to long term poverty. The drug convinces the body that the person has eaten, dampening the pain of hunger, but every time a child inhales solvents it damages their brain and the damage is irreversible. Over time, the child becomes addicted to the intoxicating smell of the drug and will sell everything they own just to buy a small amount. Sometimes, as is the case with harder drugs, they will deal in the substance in order to make a small profit to buy their own. This creates more addicts and usually younger ones. The ultimate result of this abuse over time is permanent brain damage, coma, and even death.

I learned that it is mandatory for suppliers and distributors of this rugby to add a substance to it prior to sale to change the smell, preventing the addiction. However, many distributors don't do this as they are making their living from selling this substance. Some even show the children how to cover up the bottle to make it look like something else. It is very cheap for the children to buy and, as they are usually in groups with older boys, the older ones buy the substance and distribute it to the group, although they will never admit this for obvious reasons. When a child does manage to stop inhaling the solvents, their skin can continue to smell of it for up to a year as it seeps out gradually through their pores.

Naively I at first thought that if only the boys could be told about the damage they were doing to their bodies and minds they would reconsider this lifestyle choice. I wanted to get information to them to educate them about the dangers of inhaling solvents as I believed this would really make a difference. However, later when we had a translator, I did tell them. Their response "We already know" and from one boy, aged 12, "I don't know why I'm still alive." Then it hit me; these boys didn't care. They didn't care about their lives or their future or anything apart from the next 24 hours. They didn't care whether they lived or died because their lives were intolerable and they were just trying to make it through each day. It took me a while to really accept this, as it was just so alien to anything I had experienced before. When it sunk in, I was devastated by the realisation that these children had no hope and no plans for the future; they were just waiting to die.

Soon after this, we were at the bridge one day and the large group of boys was underneath. Today they were making more noise than usual, attracting my attention. Most of the younger boys were naked after swimming in the river and had gathered in a circle. I heard loud cries from one of the boys, as if he was in real pain. The crying continued for about five minutes. I became really upset as I was convinced there was some type of assault occurring on one of the younger boys. I tried to forget this incident, but couldn't put it out of my mind and had to leave the bridge before the end of my shift.

Others told me that I must move past this, as it was the devil trying to stop me from being involved in the evangelism on the bridge. But I couldn't accept that several of us had just stood there on the bridge hearing this crying and not doing anything about it. I kept thinking that had it been in England someone would have gone to investigate and put a stop to it. But in the Philippines the boys are invisible to most local people and so they just ignored them, besides making comments about "dirty rugby boys, always causing trouble" and the like. I prayed that God would help me to overcome my fears as I returned to the bridge the following day.

3: The Bridge Team

I regularly worked at the bridge with Nick from Georgia (not in America,) whom the boys called "Sir Nick" and Thabo from South Africa, whom they called "chocolate" because he is black. We tried to explain to them that they shouldn't say this but of course this just made them say it even more. I don't think children in the Philippines understand the concept of racism and, in any event, Thabo just thought it was funny. They called me "Ma'am Natalie" but pronounced all the syllables of my name separately with a lilt at the end "Na-taa-leee." The "Ma'am" started off as a term of respect, but over time became more like "Mum," despite my frequent reminders that I was not.

Nick and Thabo both had a heart for the ministry and the three of us were a good team. We made an early decision that we would go to the bridge regardless of the weather conditions. At the start of our ministry the country was just entering its rainy season and this resulted in some crazy moments, particularly as we were trying to sell books. When I say "rainy season" I don't just mean a bit of rain, I'm talking about typhoons, floods and tropical winds that can materialise from nothing in a matter of minutes. In fact, predicting the weather became a minor competition as it was possible to spot a tiny grey cloud on the horizon one minute and then to be plunged into a typhoon within sixty seconds. We made a plastic sheet covering for our books and spent a lot of time covering and uncovering the book table. This makeshift cover was totally insufficient for the typhoon weather, and we (and our books) often got soaked because the bridge only had a small roof cover and was open to the elements on both sides. At these times, we waited until the weather had calmed down and then dried off in the sun after an hour or so.

I recall one day trying to shelter some kids, who were soaking wet, freezing cold and poorly clothed, inside my jacket and with an umbrella which was blowing around fiercely in the wind. It was possible to shout at the top of our voices, in the midst of this weather system and not be heard, so mostly we didn't try to communicate with each other. We just attached the single umbrella that we possessed to the metal railings near the ground and hid underneath it, sometimes being forced to hold on for dear life when the wind increased.

Another time, we were caught in a typhoon when trying to move all of our books in cardboard boxes stacked high on a trolley, which was really too heavy in the first place. The wind and heavy rain roared around Nick and Thabo, as they forced me to leave them struggling with the trolley, in an exposed area of the car-park. I took cover nearby and laughed a lot, along with the many local people watching, at the ridiculous situation we were in, as the two of them finally made it to safety, completely drenched and windswept, but also laughing at their predicament. We repeatedly returned to the ship soaked to the skin, but most of the time we were still cheerful and joking around.

Having been in the Philippines longer now and knowing what these typhoons can do, I am amazed at the risks that we took, but it didn't seem like that at the time. We just decided that people needed to hear the Gospel regardless of the weather, so we took it to them. The fact that on some days we were unable to talk to anyone, due to being forced to take cover for long spells, didn't really occur to us and we did have a lot of fun with the tropical weather. Some other ship crew members and many local people thought the three of us were really crazy, as we often didn't have umbrellas. The locals called out "Ma'am, ma'am, where's your umbrella? It's raining, can't you see?" in the middle of a typhoon, which I found hilarious.

In the Philippines there are various superstitions related to getting wet and umbrellas are considered an essential item. They were regularly being sold on the bridge, but on the day that I considered buying one, the unfortunate vendor's demonstration went badly wrong as he pressed the button to open it up and immediately the metal spikes pierced the material all the way round. At least he saw the funny side as I determined not to buy one. Another time Nick accidentally hit a man full in the face with one as he gesticulated wildly whilst telling a story. The man was really angry saying "Next time....!" (as if Nick planned to do it again) in a threatening tone, as Nick offered his profuse apologies. Umbrellas were generally useless due to the tropical winds, in any event, and people that carried them spent more time fighting to keep them upright without them breaking, than being protected from the rain.

Early on in the ministry on the bridge, Nick and Thabo were learning to play the guitar. This was highly entertaining as their initial efforts were painful to listen to, especially when they also tried to sing together. People pulled faces as they walked past and I put my fingers in my ears. Neither of them could start the songs on the right note, or even in the right key, but if I helped them start with the right note it generally worked out ok. Once when I came back from lunch I could see them singing from a distance so I braced myself as I got nearer, and briefly considered leaving again and returning later, but they actually sounded really good. I waited for them to finish and they both looked at me awaiting the inevitable criticism, but I had nothing negative to say as it sounded good and they had surprised even themselves.

Thankfully, they improved quickly after this and we began singing Christian songs to attract the attention of the boys under the bridge in order to try and divert them away from their solvent abuse to something more wholesome. When they came to listen, we taught them Christian songs including one in Tagalog (a language in the Philippines and pronounced Ta-gaa-log) which some of them already knew "Kay Buti Buti Mo Panginoon" (The Lord is good.) The younger boys joined in enthusiastically with this song and also "Jesus loves me this I know" which a few of them knew from attendance at Sunday School as small children. It made me sad to think that they were now so immersed in drug abuse, when they had been attending Sunday School before.

The impact on the local people was immediately obvious as the boys were transformed from dirty, naked, drug-taking, river boys, swearing and fighting, to smiling boys, fully-clothed, singing Christian songs. A local lady working daily selling food on the bridge even gave each of us a penny sweet after one such performance and told the boys their singing was beautiful.

The appearance of the guitar attracted some of the older boys especially Matthew (18) who began to come regularly for guitar lessons with Nick. He always played the song "Here I am waiting, abide in me I pray, Here I am longing for you...." (Hillsong United.) Sometimes when he was high on solvents he drifted off and played the same part over and over again or got all of the notes wrong, but at other times he played it well and the other boys gathered to listen. This made me feel emotional as the song was the story of Matthew's life. He had made a commitment to Jesus in the past and still claimed he was a Christian, but had had an ongoing battle with solvent addiction for years. We saw the struggle that he was having and it hurt to witness it and not be able to help him until he really wanted us to. His confident assertions about his faith were at times difficult for us due to the lifestyle he continued to live, but I believe he was genuinely struggling with the issues he faced and wasn't deliberately succumbing to temptations as I saw his efforts to fight against them at times.

One day we wrote "Jesus Loves You" on the arm of one of the youngest boys (whom we later discovered was Muslim) and then we saw Matthew explaining to him what this meant, a moving moment as the leaders are highly respected amongst the boys and the younger boy was really listening to him. In Filipino culture it is not embarrassing or shameful to be known as a Christian, even as a teenager, as the country has Catholic roots so most people believe in God. Coming from Western Society, this was a refreshing change for me but there were other challenges. For many people, faith in God has taken a backseat in their lives, being reduced to a formality, and a lot of the time there is no personal relationship with Jesus.

We had copies of "The Greatest Story Ever Told" in Tagalog (the story of Jesus for children told in colourful cartoon format.) We encouraged the boys to read it and explained the story to them, but their attention spans were not very good and their friends came and distracted them, encouraging them to leave to go and play or take solvents. The older boys and the ones in the middle also kept their distance from us at first as they were trying to work out whether they could trust us. If we wanted to speak to them we asked for them by name and then they came out from their hide-out, found out what we wanted, and left again. They came to play the guitar, or if they had a reason to be there, but they didn't want to just hang around with us like the younger ones did.

Thabo had been a street kid himself, so he understood the boys. Maybe for this reason he objected to them refusing to go to school and not even wanting to study, as in South Africa these things are considered a privilege. He often told the boys off for this type of attitude and the boys acted as if they were listening but weren't really paying attention. Thabo also objected when the boys took their clothes off to swim and would tell them to "Put your trousers on." He was so paranoid about this that he developed a habit of saying to them, "Don't take your trousers off, ok?" when they had just arrived and had no intention of doing so. This made me laugh a lot especially as the boys just looked so confused by this bizarre and irrelevant instruction.

Nick and Thabo started buying bread or other food for the boys, but I had heard from someone before that this isn't a good idea as it might make them dependent on us and then when we left with the ship I was worried that they would starve. This was a genuine belief, as I didn't want to cause more harm than good. But Nick and Thabo told me that God would look after them when we left and I realised that they were right. So my resistance lessened and I sometimes also bought them food. However, I was a bit frustrated one day when I saw them feeding the bread we had bought them to the fish in the river. Their explanation: "The fishes are hungry too!"

Sometimes the boys bought soft drinks which the vendors placed in plastic bags for drinking through a straw so that they (the vendor) could keep and recycle the bottle or glass (a common practice in the Philippines.) But mostly the boys took the remains of the food and drink that people passing by were carrying by tugging on them until they let go. Most people let go rather than getting into a struggle and some people felt sorry for them and gave things willingly.

One of the annoying things the boys did constantly was to ask us for our water when we had just purchased a new bottle. We couldn't really say no as they acted as if they were dying of thirst, and then the Bible verse inconveniently popped into my head about refusing to give someone water being the same as refusing Jesus. The problem was that sensibly we could only allow them to drink the remains when we had finished with the bottle due to the risk of disease. In the end we resolved this by buying two bottles and giving them one to share. This was especially necessary when we had played games with them and they had been running around and were hot and dehydrated as we couldn't then refuse to give them water.

Most of the boys were smoking in addition to sniffing solvents. The street vendors sold the cigarettes individually from the packet which was a new concept for me. I didn't make too much fuss about the boys smoking because I was more concerned about the solvent abuse which occurred much more frequently with greater damage to their short term health. Some might disagree with this stance, as the children were very young, but I knew that these vices could be dealt with later if they left the street. I am an ex-smoker and only gave up when my whole lifestyle totally changed when I became a Christian. I resented criticism of my lifestyle choices at that time as I didn't want people to judge me. I felt that if I told the boys off every time I saw them smoking it would create an unnecessary barrier at this stage so it wasn't my priority. Having said that, I made it clear I didn't like it, and we made them move away from our book-table when smoking, which most of the time they respected.

I knew that I was still holding back in some ways as I felt myself getting emotionally attached to the boys. I was worried about the impact, both for me and for them, when we inevitably left with the ship. This was exacerbated as we didn't know exactly when we were leaving since the dry dock work kept being extended. Thabo and Nick encouraged me to open my heart to really care for and love the boys. After removing my mental resistance and fear, I did. And the result was life changing.

4: The Leaders

After a while, I met our first female who seemed to be in a relationship with one of the older boys. Rachel (16) wasn't a street girl as she had a job, and I believe she had a house to live in, but she was sometimes with the boys. I gave her a wristband after sharing the Gospel with her. It had the text "The Lord is my Shepherd" on it and I explained what this meant. I expected her to keep this and look after it as it was a gift from a foreigner, which normally would be cherished and valued.

White foreigners are treated with great respect and admiration, sometimes to the point of embarrassment. Filipino females often use whitener and other products to try and make themselves more white/Western. This is ironic, as many Westerners spend a lot of time and money sunbathing or using sunbeds to make themselves more brown! Filipino's, especially the younger people, have totally unrealistic expectations of Western Countries, imagining them as some kind of paradise, mostly due to the comparative wealth and things they have seen in movies or on the TV. I tried to put a dampener on this by explaining to people that my country had many problems and that it wasn't any more beautiful than the Philippines, not wanting them to waste their time saving their money, and pining for something that would disappoint. Actually, it was a case of the "grass always being greener on the other side." Filipino's have a lot of great things that Westerners are often missing; community spirit, close family relationships and respect for the elderly/authority figures being some of the obvious examples.

However, in relation to my gift to Rachel, the next day, Rachel's boyfriend Jacob was wearing the wristband. Jacob was pretty annoying as, although he was 17, he kept putting his arm around me and trying to cuddle me. I told him not to, but he complained that the other boys did it. I said "They are just children," pointing at the 12 year olds. "You are 17." He was often hanging around all day irritating us by lying in the way or taking our books. Then he hid his flip flops underneath something to beg from the passers-by so that they would see he had no shoes on and feel sorry for him. (Unfortunately this was a tactic used by many of our boys.) I got annoyed with him many times and told him to put his shoes on and stop begging and misrepresenting himself, but I also prayed with him and encouraged him to look for work.

During our first month, Jacob left the bridge, and I didn't see him again until a few months later, when I was walking in the city and I heard "Hey Ma'am Natalie." I looked up and saw Jacob standing on the back of a Jeepney working as a conductor. A Jeepney is a metal bus without windows that serves as the local public transport in the Philippines, which my Dad affectionately termed a "rust bucket." Filipinos squash as many people as possible into these vehicles sometimes with additional   people hanging illegally onto the back. Most Westerners are surprised to see that many Jeepneys have large painted signs reading "Jesus Loves You" or "God is With Us" and similar statements due to the Catholic roots of the country. They also have crosses and various other religious artefacts hanging at the front of the vehicles. Quite a contrast to England where it's possible to get investigated, disciplined, and sacked for wearing a cross to work!

I spoke to Jacob briefly on Facebook, after I had seen him on the Jeepney, and asked how he was doing but received no reply. Most of the boys have internet access through the internet cafes on a daily basis. It costs just 15 pesos (about 20p) an hour. The next day at the bridge there was a commotion as Jacob and Rachel arrived together in nice clean clothes, and clearly having been solvent-free for some time. They walked straight past the other boys who were looking on in surprise and walked straight up to me. Jacob shook my hand and I told him it was good to see him. He nodded, smiled, and then immediately turned around with Rachel and left again. The other boys tried to approach them and talk to them, but Jacob waved them away from Rachel and the two of them then walked away, with a purposeful stride, as if they were gangsters or something. It was quite surreal, but I think Jacob was just responding to my Facebook message by showing me that they were doing well. I was pleased to see them.

One day, a large group of maybe ten or fifteen of the boys, including some of the older ones, came rushing towards us through the covered area on the bridge. They were like some kind of tornado and were shouting and laughing! They reached our table and I was afraid for a minute that they would destroy everything or steal all of our books. But they just rushed around picking up books, looking at them, and putting them back again. I tried desperately to remember some of the names from previous occasions, but failed in my efforts with the exception of one of the older boys who I knew was called David (21 years.) I believed him to be one of the leaders of this group and I could see a craziness in his eyes and behaviour that made me slightly afraid of him. I had also seen him present at the possible assault of one of the younger boys and this incident was still on my mind so I was wary of him.

David was in the centre of the tornado, whooping and shouting at us with nothing intelligible. He was obviously high on solvents as his eyes were glazed and unfocused. I didn't know what to do and felt pretty awkward, but I decided to try and say something to him as he was obviously the centre of this group. I looked into his eyes and said, "Jesus loves you David." He looked back at me and for a second his face was serious. I saw he wanted to believe it. He said, "Jesus loves me?" and I said "Yes he does; he loves all of you." David then started shouting, "Jesus loves me, Jesus loves me" in a mocking way and all of the boys laughed. I felt a bit stupid and wasn't sure if I'd said the right thing. The tornado of boys then disappeared, leaving us dazed and confused.

The next time we saw David was during a clothing distribution. He was quiet and grateful for the clothes, saying "thank you" which was a surprise. He had also somehow acquired the wrist band with the text "The Lord is my Shepherd "which I had given to Rachel and was wearing it around his ankle. I was a bit confused but I knew by this point that things got passed around the group and I thought maybe he had taken it as he was one of the group leaders. At one point, I bought wristbands for all of the boys and when David came to receive his I pointed down to his ankle at the one he had already acquired. I waited with some trepidation, expecting him to get really angry and demand his individual gift. To my surprise he just smiled, said "okay," and left.

I saw David again when one of the younger boys was ill and we wanted to send him back to his family to recuperate. (Although these boys are sleeping on the street many of them do have homes and families locally. They have run away or been forced to leave for a variety of reasons including abuse, neglect and poverty.) Nick suggested we find one of the group leaders and advise them that we were sending the boy home since it might cause trouble for him later if he was involved in some sort of street Fraternity and we just removed him from it. So we went to find one of the leaders and then we saw David in the street. He was really friendly and helpful and said it was no problem for the boy to go home. I was surprised, but I had noticed him softening towards us over time.

We didn't see David after this for a long time. But whenever I asked where he was his friends told me that he was working. I didn't really believe this as it sounded unrealistic. David had been in and out of Rehab for his solvent abuse for many years and probably hadn't held a job for longer than a few weeks at a time. Also when I asked the boys about individuals who were missing they would often tell me that this boy or that boy was "dead" and indicate a slitting of the throat motion before laughing when I looked shocked. Their information was not that reliable, especially when the "dead" boy turned up a few days later apparently having suffered no ill effects from the throat slitting. But whenever I asked after David the information was always the same and it started to come from more reliable sources like Matthew or one of the other leaders. So I asked Matthew, "Is David really working and has he changed?" He just looked at me and quietly nodded.

I believed in my heart that something important had happened in David's life, but there was no confirmation for some time. One day, he contacted me on Facebook chat. After initial exchanges I said "God bless you" and he wrote "God is good, all the time" which I was surprised to see, and then "Ma'am Natalie...you save my life.....thanks" I tried to respond and get back in touch with him but he had logged off, so I had to wait for longer to find out what had actually happened. Shortly after this I had a proper online chat with him and he confirmed that he was working. He also said that he had realised that God loved him and had given his soul to God. I asked him if he was attending a church and he confirmed that he was going to a local Baptist Church and he named the Pastor. I was so encouraged. I only saw David one more time near the bridge and he literally came for five minutes to talk to someone else working on the bridge. I spoke to him briefly and shook his hand, but he said he had to leave as he was working so I couldn't really talk to him. I could see that he was solvent free and wearing clean clothes. The craziness had gone from his eyes and he had put on some weight. I think he realised the dangers of old temptations near to the bridge so I didn't really expect to see him again.

About six months later, I saw David walking in the city on his way to the mall. I barely recognised him as he was clean and wearing nice clothes. The biggest difference was definitely in his eyes as they were bright and cheerful and he was smiling during our whole conversation as he shook my hand. The drug-induced haze was nowhere to be seen and he confirmed that he was still working at the same job and was attending the church. It was indeed a miracle and I felt my heart soar as I continued my journey.

A considerable period of time later, I was saddened to hear from David's friends that he was drinking and abusing solvents again. His friends said they also believed he had really changed as for a year or so his life was visibly different. Leaving that kind of lifestyle behind will not be easy for David and he will have temptations and trials that he may fall victim to along the way. His initial transformation was so drastic and seemed to occur almost independently of our bridge ministry. I believe he needed to know that someone loved him and cared about his life. I think when he realised that God was that person that triggered the change. I hope and pray that it was a genuine miracle of the Holy Spirit in David's life and that he is truly born again and will turn back to God.

We encouraged all of the older boys to find work and had various successes from time to time, but mostly they would work for a while and then lose their jobs and come back to us again. This was always disappointing, but I realised it was because their lives and hearts hadn't really changed, only their temporal circumstances. James (20) was one older boy who worked for longer periods of time, but always lost his job in the end. One day he came to the bridge carrying hot food that he was selling and smiling cheerfully. I purchased some food from him and was so happy to see the smile and the absence of drugs. I believed it was an answer to our prayer of only a few days before. A week later, James lost his job after a fight and was back with us looking downcast again, but we kept persevering and praying for him and the other boys.

The stories of some of the older boys are a good illustration of the emotional ups and downs we faced on a daily basis when working with these boys. There was the excitement of seeing the initial changes, and then the disappointment of the failure, sometimes just a few days later. It really reminded us, that God had to do the work in the hearts of the boys, and that we couldn't accomplish anything life-changing in our own strength. "Humanly speaking, it is impossible. But with God, all things are possible." Matthew 19 vs 26

5: The Young Ones

I grew particularly close to some of the younger boys Reuben (12) and Joshua (10) because they were young and I couldn't stand to see them inhaling solvents. Reuben especially wanted me to play games and run around with him. When he saw me coming down the street, he had developed a habit of running towards me shouting, "Ma'am Natalie" and then jumping into my arms. He was small enough to do this, and very childlike in many respects even though he was 12. Sometimes he grabbed my hand shouting "Tara na!" which means "Let's go" and then started running along the bridge, dragging me with him. I responded, "Where are we going?" But there was no reply; he just liked to play games. He often put on my jacket and strapped on my rucksack, both of which were far too big for him, then paraded around with them on and had pictures taken. He brought a kitten to the bridge one day and spent all day playing with it. He didn't seem as interested in the solvents as the others and sometimes stayed with us all day without inhaling any solvents. He just lay under our book table, sleeping or playing quietly. He was funny as well and joked around with us.

The only boy coming regularly to the bridge but not inhaling solvents was Noah (9). We discouraged him from hanging around with the group, but his mother was working nearby and, as the schooling hours in the Philippines are limited, he came in his free time. He was often bullied by the other boys who hit and pinched him, making him cry. The boys showed no mercy in this respect and little sympathy for each other's distresses unless they were serious. Noah kept us all entertained with his antics, hiding himself completely in a cardboard box and popping out suddenly or dancing on Thabo's feet as Nick played the guitar for them. The boys frequently asked us for candy which could be bought on the bridge from the street vendors for 1 peso (1.4p) each. Sometimes Noah bought two sweets keeping one for himself and giving one of us the other one. This was a nice gesture as he didn't really have much money and the other boys often bought cigarettes for 1 peso instead of buying candy and sharing it.

From time to time I saw another boy Malachi (9.) He didn't appear to be using solvents (although this changed later) and he wasn't really part of our group of boys but just showed up occasionally. When I first saw him, he was sporting a black eye and had lifted his T-shirt up over his shaved head covering it completely so that only his face was visible. His arm was linked through a friends', and he was hobbling along with a limp, looking as if he was really ill and needed help. On talking to him, I found that he wasn't ill at all and that this was just a ploy whilst begging. I'm sure it worked because Malachi was very cute. Unfortunately he also had a tendency to provoke the older boys into fights and once I had to spend an entire day trying to protect him from some of the older boys he had angered. He was clinging to the railing next to our table crying and the older boys kept trying to drag him away to hurt him in some way but I wouldn't let them. It was pathetic really as these boys were twice his age but were still intent on getting revenge.

Another day, I was sitting on the floor by the book table feeling a bit down when I heard a commotion and then various small boy voices. I listened and could hear, "Natalie, Natalie,

Natalie" over and over again. I waited for the boys to appear and then saw Nick with Reuben, Joshua, and Noah (three of the youngest boys) draped over his arms, excitedly jumping up and down. We had moved our table that day, due to the heat, so they hadn't known where we were. Nick just said, "Yes, yes. There she is!" and they ran over to me, immediately cheering me up with their obvious enthusiasm. Reuben and Joshua then fell asleep sitting on either side of me, leaning their heads on me, with my arms around their shoulders. But, I could smell the solvents on their breath and it made me especially sad because they were so young. I told Joshua that he would die if he continued this behaviour, but he just mocked me repeating, "You'll die" over and over again in a silly voice.

I tried to look after Joshua as he was the youngest boy addicted to solvents. I became aware that he was Muslim after a while as he started saying, "No Jesus, no Jesus" whenever we spoke about Jesus. The others also confirmed he was Muslim. He became upset with me on one occasion and I didn't really know why due to the language barrier. He seemed to think I was upset with him as well and that there was a problem of some sort, but I didn't know what it was. Eventually, he threw a gift I had given him in the river whilst I was watching him. The other boys suggested it might be because he was Muslim and didn't like us talking about Jesus.

Later a Filipino friend named Jude stopped by and I finally had the translation necessary to work out what was wrong with Joshua and to share the Gospel properly with the other boys. Joshua told Jude that we were fighting and that we were angry with each other. I said that that wasn't the case and that I loved this boy and the other boys but that I was sad that he threw the gift in the river. Jude thought the misunderstanding was funny as it seemed a bit ridiculous that an adult female foreigner was "fighting" with a small boy. He told Joshua that we weren't fighting as I was his big sister. Joshua seemed surprised that I wasn't angry and then gave me a hug and it was all forgotten. These were the daily frustrations we faced at first due to having no translation. I shared the Gospel with the boys through Jude and then prayed with them. All of the boys really listened and I believe that one of them accepted Jesus into his heart on this day.

6: Department of Social Welfare and Development (DSWD)

The boys now regularly came to see us and our book table, having established that we were not in any way linked with the local Department of Social Welfare and Development (DSWD) whom they hated with a passion. We learned that many of the boys had spent time in Rehabilitation in Manila having been sent there by the DSWD. Some of them had been there several times but had just returned to the street upon being released. The general procedure was that every so often the DSWD had a campaign to catch all of the boys that they knew were sniffing solvents. They rounded them all up and took them to the hospital for a chest X-Ray. They kept them for a few days and shaved their heads, resulting in them looking like gangsters, I assume for identification purposes. Then they released them back to the street pending the X-Ray result.

If the X-Ray showed that they had been inhaling solvents, they applied for a Court Order to send them to Rehab for a minimum of eight months. If the boys arrived in Rehab part way through a school year (June-March) they had to remain for the entire year. The worst case scenario, as one of our boys discovered, was if they were captured in January or February, they would probably have to remain for the end of that school year and the whole of the following year. Needless to say the Rehab centre, which is meant for adults, was not a popular place. Now, having been there many times to date, I can see why.

At first, I didn't really know anything about the DSWD. All of the information I had was from the boys and they were obviously biased. To begin with we decided not to work in conjunction with the DSWD as it seemed to be the only way to build friendships with the boys. If they had thought we knew or were associating with their enemies they would not have come near us. As I had never met the Social workers and had no idea what their attitudes or working practices were like apart from the tales of the boys, I started subconsciously to dislike the organisation and think that they were just trying to cause trouble for the boys. Later I learned that this was completely wrong and that many of the social workers had a deep love and concern for the boys as individuals and that they knew a lot about them. Also that some even went to the lengths of taking boys into their own homes to give them some respite from the street.

Nevertheless, I reassured the boys that we would not take them to DSWD or tell DSWD of their whereabouts. It did seem to me that the DSWD's practices were ineffective at times as many of these boys had already spent lengthy periods of time in Rehab but were still on the street and others were repeatedly removed from the street only to be returned a few days later. On the few occasions that we did cross paths with DSWD on the street, the boys ran away and the staff gave up looking for them straight away.

I think I was also influenced by one of the Social workers that I met at City Hall in Olongapo one day. I went to see her as one of the boys had asked me to trace his birth mother and had given me his mothers' details. However, the Social Worker didn't seem interested in helping at all and almost laughed at the request, saying that it would be impossible. I couldn't believe that she wasn't even willing to try, as it was such an important request, but when she heard it was for a "rugby boy" and the name of the boy she started talking about Rehab and a Court Order being processed and almost seemed pleased as if this was some sort of achievement. She and her colleagues then spent the next half an hour running down the "rugby boys", talking about how bad they were and that they were a blemish on society. I tried to keep my patience, but I didn't want to listen to all this, as it confirmed my suspicions and the attitudes I had already seen from many local people. These boys were just a nuisance that, in the minds of the authorities, would be better off in another city.

7: Dentist to the Rescue

Our first medical incident, on 23rd August 2012, involved Mark, a 16 year old boy that I hadn't seen before. I was working at the bridge book table as usual when my hand was grasped by Joel (12)who didn't say much but urgently dragged me to the side of the table a few metres away. He pointed to the ground and said "crying." I looked down and there was a boy lying curled up on the ground with his eyes closed and tears running down his cheeks. He had his hand against his cheek and was clearly in pain. I knelt on the ground next to him and asked the other boys, who by now had gathered round this scene, what his name was and what the problem was. They told me his name and that he had a toothache. I ascertained that he had had this for three months with no relief. I believed that he lived under the bridge with the other boys. I looked at this boy and felt the tears come to my eyes as I just felt so helpless and didn't know what to do. I told him I was going to pray for him and then did so.

I asked the others working with me what we could do, but they didn't have any ideas and some were reluctant to get involved as it could open the floodgates for similar requests. I could understand their point of view, because if you looked at the big picture and all of the needs you would become totally overwhelmed. I was learning to combat this by dealing with one person and one situation at a time and trying to effectively help each individual where possible. I contacted a Leader on the Logos Hope and asked if they could send one of their dentists to have a look at Mark or whether we could bring him to the ship for assistance. Unfortunately this was declined due to not having insurance to cover this type of incident. I began to feel desperate, knowing that I couldn't just leave this boy in this state. I told him to stay around the area and that I would find some way to help him. By this point I was even thinking of taking him to the nearest Dentist and shouldering the cost of treatment. The problem was that I was living on my Pocket Money from the ship which was just 20 Euros (£12.25) a month and I thought this would be insufficient.

So I went to lunch with Thabo and we were talking about Mark and the problem with his teeth and whether we could take him to a Dentist and what the likely cost would be. Suddenly Thabo exclaimed "Oh, I know a Dentist." I replied "What? Where do they work?" Thabo said, "Here in Olongapo and she's a Christian!" At this point I wasn't sure whether I was more excited that we might have a solution or more exasperated with Thabo for not having thought of this earlier. I looked at him incredulously as he continued talking, mentioning that he had her number and could text her right away! The Dentist immediately agreed to see Mark and dropped everything she was doing, including lunch with some friends, to rush back to her office, responding to the urgent call of duty from her missionary friends. At least, this was what she posted on Facebook later, even showing photos of her friends looking startled and her half eaten lunch in the restaurant. I then went to find Mark and tell him of our success, but he was not to be found. I was so frustrated, having got this far only to find our patient missing! None of the boys were around, so I assumed he had gone with them.

As a last resort, I decided to check under the bridge where the boys took their solvents every day. This was a bit of an intrusion as on principle we never went under there to avoid invading their private space. They came to us when they wanted to and not the other way around. However, as this was important, I climbed up over the wall and along the pipe next to the river peering down under the bridge as I did so. I couldn't see anything so I actually had to go into the dark area to check properly. I was relieved when a local man appeared and assisted me and even came under the bridge with me for translation purposes if there was anyone there. It was really dark, damp and murky under there, and knowing what had probably taken place there over the years gave me the creeps. But I looked up and saw a lone boy curled up with his back to us right at the edge of the area. At first I didn't think it was Mark, but when we spoke to him he turned over and I recognised him. I told him to come with us as we were taking him to the Dentist. He seemed a bit confused as he had been sleeping, but he readily agreed to come so we climbed back out of the darkness and back onto the bridge.

I told the rest of the team that myself and Thabo were taking Mark to the Dentist. They looked a bit surprised, but agreed to cover the book table alone allowing us to leave. We wandered through the town with Mark trailing behind us. He really looked a mess with his hair sticking up and his clothes dirty and torn. He was also extremely underweight and like a skeleton with bad acne from drug abuse. I saw that many local people, in the street, acknowledged him as he followed us and seemed amused by his presence with us. He just kept his eyes down and plodded along behind us. I thought he had to be local rather than from a distant province as he had told us.

The Dentist was really friendly and helpful, and even found an extra T-shirt for Mark. She agreed to carry out the dental work for free; we could just pay for the pain killers. She extracted four of his teeth. I watched this thinking that in England, even at 16, my mum would have been there for that type of operation. I felt sad that no one seemed to care for this boy who was obviously not taking care of himself. Actually Mark's life was not at all how he presented it to us, but at this stage we didn't really know anything about him except that he was in pain and needed a Dentist. We took him back through the town, buying some ice cream and other food which the Dentist recommended. We gave him the painkillers and then left the bridge for the day feeling somewhat satisfied that we had been able to help despite the initial barriers.

We didn't see Mark again for about a week. I kept asking the other boys where he was, but they said he had gone home. I was surprised and asked them whether he had travelled for three hours to get home as that is how long he had told me it would take. I asked where he had got the money from to get there. They didn't know and didn't really understand what I was asking. A week later Mark was back, his teeth still hurting but a lot better than before. He was very high on solvents though, which upset me as he seemed to be taking more than the others and always looked unhappy.

One day, on the bridge, I heard "Ma'am Natalie" behind me and turned to see a horrible evil faced mask on the face of someone walking towards me. The person's arms were outstretched as if they were a zombie in a movie. I pulled the mask off and it was Mark. He was really high and the mask had really frightened me. I told him not to wear the mask as it was evil. I really hated to see the boys like this. I regularly told them about the dangers of the drugs, but they didn't care and wouldn't listen.

8: Consolidating the Friendships

Over time, as we turned up for our daily ministry, the boys began communicating with us more frequently and asking us questions. We also asked them where they were from and all of them told us that they were from far away provinces three or four hours minimum from Olongapo City. Most of them also said that their parents had died and that they had no family or relatives. I recall seeing the throat slitting motion with the hand and the word "patay" which means "dead" many times when asking about relatives, which mostly turned out later to be untrue. The few that admitted having family said that they had been thrown out of their houses or had run away due to physical abuse. Some even said that they would go home if they had the money to get there. They all claimed not to have attended school for a very long time. I was surprised by this, but didn't know the culture enough to question their statements at this stage.

Sometimes the boys swam in the river holding the plastic bags to their faces and inhaling the solvents at the same time, making no attempt to disguise this from the people who could clearly see from the bridge. When they appeared on the bridge, they were often high on solvents which we recognised by their glazed eyes, their extra confidence, the smell of the solvents, and sometimes even the trails of glue in their hair and on their faces. As I was getting to know the boys as individuals, I began to really hate the substance and the sight and smell of it, knowing the irreversible damage it was doing to their minds and bodies. Occasionally I thought of England and how open solvent abuse amongst children of this age just wouldn't be tolerated and that almost any adult would intervene, but this was not England and attitudes and priorities were different.

I became really attached to the boys and looked forward to seeing them every day. I had learnt their names and asked for him by name if one boy was missing on a given day. We bought them food on most days, when we could afford it, and often I would take them to the street food stand around the corner and buy them rice for 8 Pesos (11p) and some chicken to share. This was pretty funny as they all jumped on me hanging off my arms with one of them jumping on my back for a "piggy back." We probably looked a strange sight as we headed for the rice stand. Some local people still gave us looks of disgust, but I could see that attitudes were changing slowly and some people were silently encouraging our ministry to these boys.

Unfortunately, I always had to tell the boys off at these times, as whenever one boy jumped up for a piggy back from me or anyone else, another boy tried to do something to him which in England would be considered a sexual assault. I told the boys this, but they just laughed as they knew I was a police officer before. I always stopped them from doing this and told them it was wrong. The end result of this reinforcement was that eventually when one of them did this action, another would say "no....sexual assault....police!" and then do a demonstration of someone being arrested and taken away in handcuffs. I think they got the point. They also frequently started singing "Gangnam Style" and doing the dance, but I said, "Hey, there's no sexy ladies around here" which normally stopped them midway as they thought it was funny.

29

When one of the boys turned up with a bicycle, I didn't have time to wonder where it had come from as they ushered me onto the bike and I took off with one of the boys on the back. I cycled, at high speed, 100 metres into the high street before realising that I wasn't really in control as I hadn't ridden a bike for so long and had a passenger on the back. I turned around and wobbled back only to be confronted by Nick asking what on earth I had been thinking as the street was dangerous and there was a lot of traffic. I explained that I hadn't really been thinking at all as I was caught up in the excitement of the moment. Sometimes, I forgot what others might think of me and got carried along with the activities and energies of the boys as they played. They were delighted by this of course as normally I was quite serious and telling them off for various misdemeanours.

My parents visited me in October 2012 and tried to take me to a beach somewhere, but I missed the boys and wondered if they were ok. Whilst walking around with my mum in the city, we saw Adam (11) asleep on a large pipe ten metres above the river. My mum was worried he would fall off onto the rocks below but I had seen others sleeping there before so I reassured her. Then I saw the rest of the boys swimming in the river and when Simon (12) saw me he shouted from the river "Ma'am Natalie, I miss you!" as I had been gone for a few days.

I resolved this by taking my parents to the bridge for a few hours to meet the boys. The boys kept asking my mum and dad for their names and ages and then repeated them out loud over and over again whilst pointing at them. They weren't aware that this is quite rude in England and my parents didn't mind. The boys then acquired water pistols and kept squirting us until one of them accidentally got my mum. He looked embarrassed and was preparing mentally for the shame of being told off, but his face was a picture and the real shock came when my Mum got the water pistol and squirted him back!

The next day my parents told me that, on the way back to their hotel, they had been approached by a young boy who they thought they might have met earlier with me. He just smiled and said, "Natalie is my mummy" and my mum didn't have the heart to correct him. I knew who this boy was because his family lived on the Subic Bay side of the bridge. He wasn't part of our regular group and wasn't abusing solvents. I often saw him wandering around collecting plastic recyclables in a large bag. When I first met him, he was with his cousin and I showed them an Evangecube which we sometimes used to share the Gospel. When he saw Jesus on the cross he started crying and later when he left he shouted at the top of his voice "Jesus loves me!" over and over again.

9: Practical Help

I tried to think of other ways to help the boys as they frequently asked us for food, clothes, and money. We refused to give them money as it can so easily be used to buy solvents. What we didn't realise initially is that most things are easily saleable on the street in the Philippines. The boys clothes were always ripped, torn and dirty and they "washed" them in the dirty river. They tried to persuade us to give them 10 Pesos (14p) for a shower but as we couldn't guarantee where the money was going, we declined. We later learned that the boys deliberately rip their clothes to let the air in as it is hot. They wore long baggy T-shirts down to their knees and made belts for their shorts out of anything lying around. Sometimes their shorts would develop big holes and become indecent, at which point we insisted on buying new ones for them.

I asked the ship leaders whether we could give the boys any clothing. The Book Fair manager suggested old Book Fair uniforms which happened to be the same as the uniform we were wearing to the Bridge every day. I took a whole load of the T-shirts, which were maroon with a Logos Hope logo on them and the shorts/trousers which were beige. The boys came immediately to the fence area when they saw I had something to give them and started trying them on. There was some bickering requiring intervention so I made sure the clothes were evenly distributed. A few minutes later the local police appeared to ask if we had been robbed as they had seen the boys wearing our clothes. A female police officer expressed sympathy for the boys and advised me that she was trying to find some space for them in an Orphanage. I didn't say anything but thought to myself "Good luck keeping them there. These boys won't stay anywhere they don't want to." I knew that some of them had already run away from some Christian Homes with good reputations in the area.

The boys looked really smart as they paraded around in their new uniforms. I watched them coming and going and walking in a line back and forth along the pipe leading under the bridge. It was really quite funny to see and the locals were also amused. A few hours after the distribution, Nick, who was on his day off, came running up to me looking a bit angry and confused. He said, "I just ran into some of the boys wearing Book Fair uniforms!" He had questioned them asking, "Where did you get these? Did you steal them?" And the boys had given the standard response to a foreigner when they don't understand: "Yes." I started laughing and explained what had happened, apologising for forgetting to tell the rest of the team, as they hadn't all been working when I had the idea.

Later, I also bought them wrist bands that said "The Lord is my Shepherd" and presented them to each of the boys in turn explaining that whenever they read it they should remember that Jesus was watching over them and looking after them and that they could pray to Him anytime they wanted. They lined up eagerly to receive the bands which they wore around their ankles. I had written their names on them and also made a list of the boys and their names and ages. Later I asked ship crew members to sign up to pray for each boy individually and sent an email with a similar request to the UK. I tried to email people with updates about their individual boys to keep them interested and praying.

The boys liked being treated as individuals, which was why learning their names had been so important and really helped us to connect with them. The wrist bands gradually disappeared over the next days, although some of them kept them for longer periods and they asked us for new ones whether they had one already or not. I learnt that no matter what we gave them they always asked for more. Yet it wasn't always that they wanted the thing they were asking for, they just wanted to see if we would give it to them, so we had to be disciplined in saying "no" at times.

We also gave them hoodies which we obtained from the ship since we knew they were sleeping on the street. These would be helpful to keep the noise out and more comfortable than cardboard boxes. But these, and the Book Fair uniforms, also disappeared over time. Eventually we asked one of the older boys what was going on and he told us that all of the clothes were being sold. I asked another boy why they were doing this and he just said, "We didn't need them." Sometimes what we thought they needed was very wrong. I was so desperate to help these boys that I was forgetting that this couldn't always be done in material ways. I started thinking, "How much money will it take to get these boys off the street and off drugs?", but I was convicted by the Bible verses

Psalm 49 vs 7-9 "No one can redeem the life of another or give to God a ransom for them—the ransom for a life is costly, no payment is ever enough—so that they should live on forever and not see decay."

I read these verses twice in separate places shortly after I began thinking like this. However, these experiences were also good for us as we could see what was helpful and what wasn't, and it was only through our mistakes that we learnt.

My own clothes from the ship started to deteriorate and, instead of replacing them, I used the holes to deal with the boys' demands. When they said, "Ma'am Natalie, give me T-shirt." I said "No, you give me T-shirt!" pointing to the holes in my clothes. They laughed at this and didn't ask me again. As I mentioned before, sometimes they weren't interested in getting the items. They wanted to test our care for them and they saw this in monetary terms. We had to learn to understand this and be wise when spending money.

10: Internet Access and Social Media

As I briefly mentioned earlier, another thing that surprised us is that these boys all had access to the internet and Facebook accounts. They spent a large amount of their time online after begging in the street to get the money. The internet is pretty cheap and they liked to play computer games online. Sometimes they played the games all night as some internet cafés are open 24/7. Internet addiction is a big problem in the Philippines with large numbers of children spending most of their free time in the internet café's where they can surf online virtually unmonitored for as long as they like. This is a particular problem during their school holidays as there aren't too many alternative options and many parents are working long hours just to put food on the table. I even witnessed young boys watching a pornographic video in the middle of the day in one of the café's. It was only switched off when I notified the manager. Some, but not all, of the café's do ban children from entering during school hours. Violent and addictive videos games like Defence of the Ancients (DOTA) and World of Warcraft are visible on nearly every screen on entry to these Café's, as children eagerly line up to wait for their turn.

I first learned that our younger street boys had internet access when I was walking along the street and suddenly saw three of them descending a staircase and stepping out into the street in a huddle. I asked them what they were doing as they looked extremely suspicious and they said, "Internet café ma'am." I was shocked by this as I had believed that they didn't have enough money to eat, but now I saw them wasting money in the internet café. I had to learn that things are not always as they seem in this respect.

This is something that many people in the UK have asked me about so I will try to explain why this happens. It is best illustrated like this; one day one of the boys named Joel, whilst begging, received 1000 pesos (£14) from a foreigner. This is a lot of money for an adult, who may earn just 200(£2.71) pesos a day as a security guard, let alone a child. A street meal can cost as little as 30 pesos (41p.) Joel returned to the group triumphantly waving his riches. I thought to myself, "Great, now we won't have to feed them for a week and then maybe some of them won't take drugs either." Wrong! Just a few minutes later Joel excitedly went into the city with a few of the other boys and returned an hour later with several fake guns. The money had gone. Joel didn't even think about buying food for that day, let alone future days or weeks.

These are young boys that haven't been taught money management skills and who haven't had access to toys or other material things. If they get money, they will buy toys or games, or spend it on computer games on the internet, guaranteed. The thought of saving the money for food isn't exciting for a teenage boy, but impressing his friends with the latest gadget definitely is. Food isn't even a consideration until it becomes a necessity and they recognise that unless they eat soon they will collapse. It's sad, but the boys know that they can stave off the hunger pangs with solvents later on and that this is cheaper than buying food, so this is what they do. They honestly don't think about anything except the next few hours in front of them. They have no plans and no future. Part of the reason is because they have become invisible to people and they are just crying out for attention. They are crying out for someone to notice them, for someone to take an interest in them as individuals, to spend time with them, to really get to know them and not then to disappear from their lives. They need, as we all do, to matter to someone, to be cared for and loved by someone.

11: Living at the Hospital

Inevitably, spending a lot of time with the boys every day resulted in us having to deal with various medical incidents that cropped up. The system in the Philippines is that you can only receive treatment at the hospital if you can pay for it, even in an emergency. Clearly, the boys were never going to be in a position to pay for any type of treatment. Often the security guards at the entrance to the hospital wouldn't even let them in through the front door, let alone establish what was wrong with them or whether it was urgent. This is just another example of how these children have become invisible to local people. They are seen by those in authority as a "nuisance" or a "shame" on society and no one really knows what to do with them. I think the authorities wish they weren't there and would go somewhere else, a bit like the police in England who sometimes move homeless people on from one town to another, which doesn't deal with the root of the problem.

It was a real blessing to have the Christian charity "Helping Hands Healing Hearts" stationed within the local hospital, which itself was only a five minute walk from the bridge. Amongst other things the charity helped financially if a person couldn't afford treatment. We often went begging to their office with one of our boys in tow to ask for help. They knew all of the boys we took to them from previous incidents and often knew where they lived and things about their lives. I became suspicious of the stories the boys had told us at this point. They were clearly local, although they had told us they lived a long way away in Manila and other far off lands!

Sometimes we felt as if we were living at the hospital as we were so frequently in attendance. The problem was that if we had to take one boy there then some others suddenly developed illnesses or cuts/scrapes that hadn't been a problem to them before that needed attention. We ended up taking a herd of them all together which caused further problems as they fought and jostled with each other in the waiting area or disappeared outside to smoke when their name was being called.

In the early days, one of our regular boys Solomon developed a high fever. We were alerted to this by Joel, the same boy that had grabbed my hand and dragged me to Mark. He knew that we would help if we could. Solomon was lying on the floor and was very hot. Again, I prayed for him and didn't really know what else to do. Joel was crying as he said he didn't want Solomon to die. I told him that he wouldn't die, but I didn't really know what would happen as I thought he might have contracted some kind of disease in the river as it was polluted. We let him rest for a few hours and kept an eye on him, but his temperature wasn't going down and he was becoming less coherent. So, myself and Nick took him to the hospital.

We sat for hours waiting for various tests and eventually decided to visit "Helping Hands" who immediately offered to help us with the financial cost of the medicine. They also knew Solomon already and told us that he lived locally in a poorer part of town in a mountainous area and that he had eight siblings and the family didn't have enough food. Solomon then admitted that he had run away to find food and stayed on the street when he got involved with the "rugby boys." He agreed to go home for one week to recover. He was given anti-biotics and we took him for a meal afterwards. The problem was that as soon as the other boys saw us back in the street they wanted to accompany us for the meal. As we had little money and didn't want to start a trend, we advised them that this was a special treat for Solomon as he was sick and that he would be going home afterwards to rest. They were all really concerned about him and accepted what we said, which was a relief.

After the meal, we put Solomon into a Jeepney and made sure he knew how to take his medicine. He still had a fever and we worried about sending him home when we didn't know what sort of reception he would get, but it was impossible for us to accompany him at that time of the evening without knowing where to go or how to get back, so we prayed for him instead. He promised that he would stay at home for at least a week to recover. We spent a lot of time telling him about Jesus and encouraging him to go back to school. We were hoping we wouldn't see him again on the bridge.

Unfortunately, on arrival the next day, there was Solomon's cheeky face grinning at us. I went straight over to him saying, "What are you doing here?" but he just grinned as if it was fine and the other boys also were laughing. At least he no longer had a temperature and seemed well again. But then I saw his medicine bottle was empty and the tablets had gone. These were meant to last for a whole week! He indicated that all of the other boys had shared them with him. I realised then how dangerous it is to give a group of boys already experimenting with drugs any type of medicine, expecting them to take it properly. Learning from this experience, next time, we kept the medicine ourselves and gave it to the boys as necessary. Shortly after this however, Solomon disappeared from the bridge never to return, and his friends advised that he had gone back to school.

Another accident, which I didn't really want to deal with directly, occurred under the bridge. One of the boys came running, shouting "Accident! Accident!" I went to have a look and could see that Joel had fallen and that his bone was partially protruding from a gash on his ankle area. I couldn't deal with this and knew I didn't have to as there were other people working with me. Nick helped Joel to the hospital where the doctor said that it was just as well someone had brought him or there may have been a serious infection with dire consequences.

The wound required ongoing treatment, ideally daily at the hospital, but we knew that there was no way Joel was responsible enough to attend a daily appointment. To deal with this situation, now that we were self-appointed medical experts, we purchased very basic supplies of alcohol, cotton wool, bandages, and some kind of antiseptic cream. Then we told Joel that he had to come and see us every day to get the dressing changed. We did this every day for a week and were grateful when, another crew member from Logos Hope, saw us attending to him on the bridge and was so moved that he offered to pay for any additional medicine. This practice also raised the attention of the passers-by who looked shocked to see white foreigners sitting on the dirty ground taking time and care to clean the wound of a street boy. The wound began to heal, but due to the conditions on the street and Joel running around it got infected and we had to take him back to the hospital.

Eventually, to my relief, our frequent cleaning, changing dressings, and prayer paid off and it healed. I was really relieved as I hadn't a clue what I was doing but had to pretend to the boys that I did, otherwise they wouldn't have trusted me to help Joel. Without intervention, he wouldn't have had any treatment, which could have resulted in serious consequences- like losing his foot!

The boys started calling me "Doctor." As I mentioned before, these boys don't think beyond the next 24 hours as evidenced by their solvent use so I was constantly afraid that at any moment Joel could say that he had had enough and that he didn't want any more treatment. However, to his credit, he obviously realised that this was serious and was sensible. We also used the medical kit to deal with many cuts and scrapes as the boys liked to feel that they had some injury or other problem worthy of our attention. Even Matthew the leader asked for attention. I used a cotton bud to clean the wounds with alcohol, then stuck some cream in it and put a bandage or band aid over the top. Simples!

12: Breaches of Trust

One of the surprises for me when working with these boys was that we hadn't had any major problems with thieving. We didn't want to put temptation in their path, but we also didn't want to have to watch over our belongings all of the time. So we trusted the boys that we knew not to go in our bags and not to take things from us. We had a few instances of theft which stand out in my mind, as it was always upsetting due to the breach of trust rather than the value of the items.

We were selling bracelets with Bible verses on them from the book table, and a few of these disappeared one day. Unfortunately, this happened at the same time that some men from one of the local Children's Home's had come to see our ministry on the bridge. I got upset and angry with the boys. The men had come to see whether any of the boys might be suitable for one of the Homes, but left shortly after the theft, advising me to be patient with the boys. Before the theft, I was already a bit disappointed by the visit as one of the older visitors had commented, "What these boys need is a bit of stick!" demonstrating a thrashing motion with his hand. Some of our older boys overheard this and turned their heads away in disgust. I thought, "This is the last thing these boys need. They have experienced enough of that at home which is why many of them are here." We had spent a lot of time working with the boys, preparing them to leave the street and the progress could have been destroyed with one careless comment.

The bracelets were later returned broken by one boy who hadn't taken them, he said very politely "Are you missing these ma'am?" as he held them out to me. I was reassured, as I realised, that the damage could have been caused by accident and that at least they hadn't been sold. The boys hadn't been taught how to look after things, so sometimes damaged them unintentionally, by handling them roughly without due consideration of the consequences. Or by fighting with each other for possession!

We did experience a theft by "one of our other boys" as it were and it really hurt me. The incident started when I caught Reuben red-handed. He was going through my purse which someone had removed from my bag, which was underneath the book table. I saw him take 2 pesos (3p) out of it and challenged him to give them back. He refused and ran off with the coins laughing and taunting me. Basically his view was that it was just 2 pesos and it didn't matter, but I wasn't going to allow this as I had to make the point that stealing even a small amount of money is wrong. I double checked my purse and saw that another 500 pesos (£7) was missing. I was 90% sure of this. I went after Reuben and challenged him about this but he became very upset and immediately gave the 2 pesos back. A local man also accused him of taking the money, but he denied it and started crying and walking around mumbling to himself and getting really upset and angry. I could see that he hadn't done it so I asked the local man to tell him that I knew he hadn't done it and to tell me who had. He didn't know.

I was upset by this point as I was hurt by the breach of trust. I went and sat away from everyone to think about what had happened and who might have taken the money. A local man saw that I was upset and tried to find out what had happened. He dragged one of the sleeping boys named Luke (15) out from under the table and started violently beating him around the head. I was distraught and tried to intervene as I knew Luke wasn't responsible since he had been asleep. I couldn't believe the level of violence being used! Luke was crying and shouting at the man through angry tears as I tried to calm the situation down.

One of the other boys came over to me and took my hand and said that they had reported the theft to the police and that I should come and talk to the police officer. I didn't really want to go as I was upset but I knew it must've been hard for the boys to approach the police. Since the officers were waiting I went to see them. The boys gathered around and some of them were as upset as I was. They were all shaking their heads and looking ashamed on behalf of their group. I noticed that one boy was missing: Joshua. When I thought about it, I knew he was the culprit, as he had left in a hurry a little earlier with no explanation. The boys were all very apologetic. I told the police that I didn't want to file a complaint but that I was hurt by the breach of trust.

I didn't go to the bridge the next day. It was one of the few occasions where I couldn't face the boys. I asked Thabo to challenge the boys and see if he could recover my money and get to the bottom of the matter. He told me that they were very subdued with no solvent abuse all day and they were very keen to sing the songs and to behave themselves. This was interesting as it proved that the boys weren't so addicted to the solvents that they had to take them every day. Thabo talked to Joshua about the incident, but he didn't admit anything. I went back the next day and Joshua wasn't around. In fact, I didn't see him for two weeks. I asked his friends where he was and they said that he was at home. I thought maybe his relatives had found out what had happened and were angry with him for thieving. I couldn't have been more wrong!

After a while, one of the boys told me that Joshua had decided to give the money back to me as he felt so guilty about it, but that his Uncle had taken the money from him and told him that if he returned it to me he would kill him! At this stage I thought things were getting a little out of control so I told the messenger to advise Joshua that if he came and said sorry to me in person that would be the end of the matter. I asked this boy why Joshua had stolen the money and was told, "You didn't need it." Actually I did need it, as it was nearly half of my pocket money for the whole month, but the boys saw us handling Book Fair money at the book table and often thought we had more money than we did. Over time, I had become friends with all of the boys on Facebook and they often contacted me online when I was on the ship to ask where I was. Joshua sent me a message on Facebook saying that he was sorry. I said that it was ok but that I wanted to see him in person.

 A few days later when I got to the bridge I saw a small figure standing at the end of the bridge with a T-shirt pulled completely up over his head so I couldn't see who it was. I thought it might be Joshua so I called out to him but he looked at me quickly through a gap in the clothing and then ran away to the other side of the fence where all the other boys were still sleeping. I decided to give him time so I carried on with setting up the table. But I kept seeing him looking at me through gaps in his clothes. I told one of the other older boys to tell him to come and say sorry to me and it would be ok, but I could see he was finding it very hard. He came nearer and nearer to the fence and I moved over to talk to him, but he kept backing away. Eventually, he removed his T-shirt a little but still wasn't saying anything so I touched his head through the fence and said to him that he should look at me and say he was sorry. After a while he did this and I said it was ok and gave him a hug. I didn't want to make a big thing of it so I went back to what I was doing, but a few minutes later I looked across and saw that he was crying quietly by himself. This incident damaged my relationship with Joshua, and although I tried, I found it difficult to go back to how we had been before.

Our final theft incident occurred a lot later in our ministry. Our bridge team had changed and there were some new crew members with me. Some new boys came that I hadn't seen before. I didn't pay them much attention as we were used to having extra boys and they seemed to know our other boys. However, after a while, I noticed one of them blatantly going through the bag of one of the crew members, seemingly making no attempt to hide what he was doing. I shouted at him and made all of the boys stay where they were whilst we checked their pockets. I was really angry, but as they didn't seem to have anything on them, and the crew members couldn't confirm that anything had been taken, we had to let them go. I think they hid the money in their underwear because some of them even pulled their shorts down to prove they weren't responsible and in protest at the accusation! Immediately after the search, the new boys ran off.

Shortly after they had gone, one crew member found that she had lost some foreign currency and some local money. Our regular boys also disappeared and, a short time later, one of them came running back to say that one of the thieves had been found and some of the money recovered. I heard a loud commotion in the street and went over to see what was going on. I saw a local man who looked pretty angry holding a boy of about 13 years by the scruff of his neck. The man said to me "Have you lost something?" and I explained what had happened. He told me that the boy had tried to present the foreign currency in his store. By this point a large group had gathered including all of our regular boys, so I took the opportunity to show mercy to this boy. I asked the man to translate then asked the boy if he was sorry. When he said yes, I advised him that we forgave him and then I told him and all the onlookers about Jesus, and how He has forgiven us for our sins allowing us to forgive others when they sin against us. It was really a great opportunity for our boys to see us put our words into practice.

Unfortunately, the new crew members were so shocked by what they had witnessed that they were reluctant to come back to the bridge! I explained that it wasn't our regular boys but I think they were just shocked by some of the behaviour and by seeing me upset when I was meant to be in charge. One female crew member spoke about the boys persistently asking her if she had a boyfriend, trying to cuddle her and jumping all over her which had upset her as she believed they were trying to assault her or touch her inappropriately.

Actually, our regular boys were always careful with us, as females, in this respect, as although there was a lot of messing around and physical contact between us and the boys, they always made efforts not to make us uncomfortable, by keeping their hands to themselves, and by not taking advantage of the freedom that we allowed them when playing games/other rough and tumble. I knew that the boys were just curious about foreigners and their white skin and different features, hence the many questions and comments. This was how they expressed their curiosity because they felt comfortable with us, so it didn't bother me, but I had to appreciate that others were different.

I was glad that the other crew members hadn't been there when our regular boys were behaving really badly, which on occasion they did. It tended to be bad behaviour as a group as they riled each other up. They begged from our customers, whilst they were browsing at the book table or hid under the table which had a cover hanging down. Then they snatched half eaten food or drinks that people had in their hands whilst looking at the books, making them jump back in shock as they hadn't even known anybody was there. Actually this was quite funny, but we dutifully told them off until one day when we didn't need to. On this day, a local man became irate when this happened to him and dragged two of the boys out from under the table shouting at them and threatening to beat them in the street. We just looked the other way and whistled, as we had been expecting something like this for a while.

13: Gang Fight and Other Trouble

People often tell me that my police background prepared me for this type of work with the street boys. At the time I didn't see it, but as I write this I can see that maybe I might be less intimidated by these boys due to my previous line of work. The difference is that in the police you are generally not emotionally involved with the people you are dealing with. Sometimes you might deal with a case where you do develop a relationship with a victim or witness due to preparation for a court case and then it is hard if the result is not what you had hoped for. But working with these boys was so much more challenging because it was impossible not to get emotionally involved due to the length of time that we were working with them for. In most cases they didn't have anyone else that really loved or cared for them. They grew to love and trust me, but they were physically damaging themselves everyday right in front of me and I was powerless to stop it. The problem is that we were involved in long term work without resources or partnerships to support us adequately. This wasn't anybody's fault; it was just how things worked out due to the ship's unexpectedly long dry dock.

One incident I recall where my police background was definitely useful was in preventing a gang fight! A mixed group of school students were crossing the road near to the bridge. One of them made a comment to one of the street boys as he probably knew him from a time when that particular boy had been in school before. But it was the wrong thing to say because suddenly all of the street boys were summoned from under the bridge, in an attempt to protect this boy's reputation, and they were carrying very large rocks. The students, now terrified and no doubt wishing they had remained silent were herded onto the bridge like cattle and cornered by the street boys and the rocks. This all happened in a matter of seconds.

At first I just stood there wondering what on earth was going on, but then I saw the expressions on the faces of some of the street boys and I realised they were really angry and were going to throw the rocks at the students. One of the rocks was twice the size of a person's head! I ran into the middle of this scene as there was about twenty metres between the two groups who were facing each other from their battle lines. I shouted at the smallest boy, Reuben, who had the biggest rock, to put it down, thinking that he would obediently obey me as I had a close relationship with him, but he ignored me completely. I then shouted for Matthew the street boy's group leader and he appeared. I shouted at him, "Matthew, you have to stop this! If Reuben throws that rock he will kill one of those kids and go to prison for the rest of his life." I couldn't believe his casual response. "No, he won't. He's a juvenile, nothing will happen." Later I learned that this was essentially true....

I was still standing between the two groups so that any rocks would hit me first. I knew that the boys wouldn't throw rocks whilst I was standing there (or so I hoped!) The amazing thing is that there were loads of adults around and no one was doing anything to resolve this problem. They were all just watching and waiting. In the end, Matthew relented and signalled to someone in the other group and called off the whole thing. The students fearfully made their way off the bridge and were chased up the street by the street boys to "see them off." I was amazed at how quickly little cute Reuben had turned into a monster, and how he had blatantly ignored me when I tried to talk to him. It was a lesson in loyalties though and demonstrated to me that their ties to each other as their "street family" were still stronger than their ties to us.

The boys were also in trouble with the local police, often for no good reason other than that they were in the wrong place at the wrong time. Several times I felt it necessary to intervene as I knew they hadn't done anything, but most of the time I couldn't be sure. Sometimes I arrived on the bridge to be told that one or other of the boys was in the police station just up the road, having been detained for theft or some other crime. The law in the Philippines, as mentioned earlier, doesn't allow for juveniles to commit a crime, so they were released after a day or two normally with stories of how they had been beaten up in the police station, which I was unable to verify.

Another day, Malachi (9,) was detained and crying outside the mall one day for allegedly stealing some food. I asked the security guard what he had done and when he told me I felt a bit angry. I knew Malachi was hungry. It sounded like he had tried to relieve someone of their left over food as they had left the mall, something lots of the boys did, but that this particular person hadn't appreciated it. I asked Malachi if he was hungry and of course he said "yes" through his tears. So I told him to stop crying and to come with me and I would buy him some food. I told the guard where I was going and off we went. After Malachi had eaten I looked over at the guard and signalled to him that we were leaving now and he nodded. I told Malachi to be on his way and not to cause any more trouble. Inside, my heart was beating fast and although I was acting and speaking with authority and confidence, I was expecting the guard just to take Malachi back into custody again, but he didn't.

Another time Isaac (11), a boy who I didn't know that well but who seemed to me to be one of the harder boys, got into some trouble in a restaurant as he was alleged to have taken someone's purse. On the few occasions that I had met or seen him before, he was alone and high on solvents. Once I saw him repeatedly trying to get a coffee from a machine, only to fall over backwards in the process. He then lay on his back on the floor as his eyes rolled back in his head and he shouted nonsense at me. I had never seen anything like this in a child, but I didn't really know what I could do to help him whilst he was in this state. In the end I had to leave, but the memory stayed with me. On a more sensible occasion, I spoke to him late at night, when he was sitting with the adult men outside a shop near to where he lived. I asked him whether he liked to be on the street and he said, "No." He said that there was a problem at home, but wasn't specific.

In relation to the theft allegation, I knew he hadn't done what was alleged. The angry tears and shouting immediately demonstrated to me that here was one unjustly accused. I tried hard not to resent the lady making the accusation, but it was obvious that she had seen this "street boy" and jumped to conclusions because "Well, that's what this type of boy does, isn't it?" I told the security that I would vouch for Isaac and led him quietly outside. But the guards were still threatening to call the police and Isaac was distraught. He picked up a rock and motioned to throw it through the window. I stood in the way and reasoned with him. Fortunately at this point the DSWD appeared and, as they are feared much more than the police, Isaac made a hasty exit. Joel, who was watching the scene, didn't run quickly enough and was detained by DSWD, only to be released a few days later. I remember the look on Joel's face pleading with us to do something as I was forced to walk away and leave him with them. We had warned them time and again that if they remained on the street they would eventually be captured and sent to Rehab but they didn't listen.

Another desperate situation relates to one of the group leaders, Matthew. I was aware that he had been in and out of Rehab over the years and that this was where he had made a commitment to Jesus, through a Christian social worker there. Matthew often asked me and other crew members for help saying that he wanted to change his life, especially during conversations online, but when we went to see him and offered to help him he changed the subject or acted as if he didn't know what we were talking about. I knew his background and family situation were traumatic as he sent me messages online about how much he hated various members of his family. He had been on the street for many years.

 On one occasion he wrote a really deep message and posted this to me on Facebook. It's too personal to reprint in full, but it was basically saying that he knew that others were disappointed with his life and that he hated himself because of what he had become and that he was trapped. However, he was inspired to change because of the examples around him and the hope that he could see. I discussed the message with the bridge team and they were surprised, Nick said "I didn't know they even thought like that." Reading the message, I saw that Matthew was trapped in a big dark hole, but that he was starting to see light at the end of the tunnel.

I contacted a Pastor friend and asked if he would be available to see Matthew at the church the following day. Then I tried to persuade Matthew to come and see the Pastor with me, but he refused. Later, the Pastor came to the bridge to meet some of the boys and had a long talk with him. Matthew was really listening as the Pastor said that he had to really make a definite decision and that then we would be able to help him. After the Pastor left, however, Matthew went back down under the bridge where he flew into a massive temper. He was shouting and swearing and cursing and crying angry tears. He inhaled drugs at top speed, threw things around and moved around in great distress. Nick went to try and help and comfort him, but in the end Matthew shoved him away.

Matthew later said that it was because, while he had been speaking to the Pastor, someone had stolen his money from under the bridge. I knew there was more to it than this as it wasn't a lot of money and we offered to replace it which he refused. It was really an extreme reaction and behaviour that we hadn't witnessed before. I wondered if it was a spiritual problem and another boy later told us something that confirmed that this was probably the case.

14: The Real Stories

The bridge team had asked the Ship Management for a Filipino to work on the bridge several times as we were struggling to communicate properly with the boys. We had built friendships and the boys trusted us, but we wanted to have deeper conversations and find ways to really help the boys longer term. Enter Arlene who joined the ship in September 2012, and joined us on the bridge soon after. This was a real blessing but also an eye opener as we started to hear the real reasons why the boys were on the street. Although they had given us their real names and some of their basic stories were true, most of the facts about where they were living and other details were lies/exaggerations.

Most of them lived in Olongapo City and had families and homes to go to. They were on the street for a range of reasons including poverty, broken homes, physical abuse, and rebellion. I believe they lied about where they were from because they thought we would try and take them back to their problem families if we knew they lived locally. They were used to lying to the police and DSWD about their lives. Sometimes this convinced the police not to take action. The police told me that they had tried to break up the group under the bridge before and had sent the boys back to the Provinces that they claimed to be from, only to have them return a few weeks later. Maybe this was because they had lied about being from the various Provinces in the first place. This also explained the mutterings I had heard before about the police having no jurisdiction over the boys. It seemed that the authorities had given up trying to break up the group which had become almost impossible to manage as they were like a large family helping and looking out for each other.

It was painful to hear the boys' stories as they were similarly traumatic. Simon said that he was embarrassed that his family was poor. Simon's parents were separated and he and his sister lived with his Dad who was disabled. Simon was collecting plastic from around the city to help his family. This is a common way for people to make a small amount of money, collecting recyclable plastic. They receive around 5-10 pesos (7-14p) for every large bag of plastic. But Simon was tired of doing this so he dropped out of school and got involved with the "rugby boys." Joel's parents were also separated and he believed that his family would never be happy unless they got back together, but his father is remarried and has three young children with his new wife. Joel told us that he was beaten and made to work long hours at home. Reuben also was beaten by his father who was cruel to him. (This was confirmed later by a neighbour.)

Adam was one of the boys that worried me the most as he had a learning difficulty making social interaction difficult. He stood next to me and punched me repeatedly in the arm whilst using profanity in English. When I told him to stop, he laughed and moved away but then started doing it again a few seconds later. Now I believe it was drug related, but at the time I wasn't sure why he kept doing this. Adam did have friends in the group but was often alone and was easily influenced to bad behaviour by some of the other boys who took advantage of his disability.

One morning I was walking in the city early at 8:30am not expecting to see any of the boys as they slept until 10/11am normally. Then I saw Adam. He was walking in the street with his hand up his T-shirt which was over his nose and inhaling from a plastic bag. He didn't see me to start with due to being high on drugs but I said his name and he looked at me. I couldn't believe no one was doing anything as it was in the city centre with many people around and it was obvious that he was inhaling solvents. I tried to persuade him to give me the bag so I could buy him some food instead but he refused and ran off. The image of Adam alone and inhaling solvents early that morning, is ingrained in my memory. It sounds crazy, but at least when they are in the group they have each other. Actually, this was one of the problems we had later: they had been in the group for so long that the group was their "family" and the street their "home."

Adam told Arlene that he had been sent to Olongapo to live with his Uncle as his parents didn't want him. He had just been thrown away like a piece of rubbish. They kept his sister. Adam just wanted a family of his own. A neighbour or his Uncle (we were unable to verify which) gave him money every day for food but he wanted to be back with his parents and to be loved by them. After he shared his story, Adam sat on the ground in the centre of the bridge, with people milling all around him heading in both directions, but no one was taking any notice of him. He was invisible. I continued to watch him as he sat there all alone. The expression of pain and anguish on his face was so real that I had to turn my face away. What on earth had happened to this boy to make him feel like that?

Luke (15) was Muslim and often took more drugs than the others because his father had died recently. He had more respect for us than some of the others, maybe just because he was a little older. I sensed his problems were genuine and that he was deeply unhappy. We repeatedly told the boys that they should go home to their houses and not stay on the street. He told us he was living nearby and I asked if we could go and see his house and meet his family. He wasn't prepared for this and came up with many excuses, but we applied gentle pressure and eventually he agreed. His friends thought this was a big joke as he was high on solvents and didn't really think we were serious. They were laughing at him when we said, "Let's go."

We arrived at Luke's house quickly as it was not far from the bridge. This was a surprise as I had believed it would be further away. We were welcomed in, although the family seemed surprised to see us as we were unexpected. I hoped Luke wouldn't get in trouble later for bringing foreign uninvited guests home, especially Christian ones! Luke's mother was there with about twenty other people including many children. They introduced Luke's brother's, who were all married, with their wives and children all living in this tiny space which looked like it consisted of just two rooms with little furniture.

One of the reasons for requesting a visit was to try and get Luke enrolled in school. For this we needed his birth certificate, so we asked his mother for this. She advised that she didn't know where it was and when we checked she didn't even know how old he was or what his birthday was. This was really upsetting as Luke just sat there watching the proceedings with a blank expression on his face as he had obviously heard it all before.

A birth certificate or a certificate of completion from the previous school year is a requirement for annual enrolment at school. Sometimes this paperwork is lost by families or destroyed during typhoons or floods. The result: The child is not allowed to enrol unless they or the parents complete a lengthy process which sometimes involves long distance travel which they can't afford! As I have discovered, the whole procedure is very frustrating and time consuming and doesn't always secure the desired outcome. Although school placements are free, many families can't afford to pay for their children's lunch and transportation to get there or they need them to earn money by working illegally, so they don't send them to school.

I was appalled that Luke's mother didn't know even basic things about him and didn't seem to really care, and that our efforts to obtain his birth certificate came to nothing. I thought to myself, "No wonder he's on the street. I think I would rather be there than in this place." It wasn't just the conditions that were tough, but the lack of care and concern from his mother. If the family really cared, they could easily have come to the bridge and taken Luke home and away from the drugs. They expressed concern about his solvent abuse to us and a few times after this visit his older brother did come to the bridge and take him home. However, the concern seemed to fade over time, as if they were just trying to satisfy us in some way.

As we left the place, I put my arm around Luke and said, "See, it was okay, us meeting your family, wasn't it?" He smiled and said that it had been fine. He was very cheerful after that, but I couldn't stop thinking about this visit and how naïve I was in thinking that if he would just go home things would be better...

15 : Mark: The Prodigal Son

One day I turned up at the bridge to find Mark (the boy treated by the Dentist before) holding his arm and indicating he was in pain. I asked him what was wrong and he said that he thought it might be broken. Noah (9) also kept spitting blood on the floor that appeared to be coming from one of his teeth and a third boy Simon (12) had developed raised lumps all over his hands overnight from some kind of allergy. I really didn't want to spend another day in the hospital, so I told them that I couldn't take them anywhere at that moment as there was no one to stay at the bridge table. Mark began crying as he was in pain, so in the end I relented and arranged cover at the book table.

At the hospital, I observed that Mark said he was "born again" when asked for his faith at the reception. He was very specific about this and made the distinction from being Catholic. I talked to Mark a lot about the Gospel whilst we were waiting and how Jesus was the only answer to the problems in his life, although I didn't know much about his life. He began crying again whilst Noah was looking on. I asked Noah if he knew why I was trying to help them and he said, "Because you are kind!" I made sure that he knew it was because of Jesus, but I was touched by his comment in any event.

Mark told me that he had spent time in rehabilitation before with a few of our other boys. He told me a lot of things about his life that were really shocking. He said he had been on the street for many years and that his ex-girlfriend's family was trying to kill him because they thought he had gotten her pregnant. I was confused by this since I had seen his profile picture on Facebook, which appeared to be a recent photo. In the photo he was in his school uniform, looking clean and a healthy weight. I challenged him about this asking, "Mark, what happened to you? You look good in your Facebook picture, and now you've dropped out of school and are on the street taking drugs?" But when I said this the tears came again, so I just reminded him that Jesus can help him. I felt really sorry for him but couldn't understand what was going on in his life or how I could help him.

In the end, Noah left the hospital before receiving treatment as he was impatient, so I got his prescription for him and gave it to his mother. Simon was told he had an allergy and was given cream. Mark had an X-ray which confirmed there was no break to his arm, but they gave him a sling for comfort purposes which he seemed to be happy with, probably due to the extra attention it would inevitably bring him. So we left after only a few hours.

Mark sometimes mentioned a church in the area by name. So I asked him if he wanted us to take him to visit the Church and the Pastor, and he said that he did. We arrived at the Church and spoke with the Pastor and introduced them. Mark agreed to come back and go to the Church on a future date. It all seemed quite easy, and a little too easy in a strange way. Later, when we were speaking about the Church and the Pastor, Mark surprised us all by saying the Pastor's name. He then told us that he already knew the Pastor that we had introduced him to because this was his previous church! This was all a bit odd as the Pastor hadn't indicated that he knew Mark at all. Mark then told us that in addition to attending the Church, he had also been going to a Bible study and had even led Sunday School. The mystery was only to deepen.

Mark became good friends with Luke, due to their age similarity, but unfortunately most of the time they were high on solvents. I was really concerned about them and their influence on each other. As they were walking in the street, Mark looked miserable and hopeless as he always seemed to. I said, "Mark, you just look so unhappy. What is wrong?" I was shocked when he just began openly crying in the street in front of Luke and passers-by. I looked away as I struggled to contain my own emotion. I could see the deep distress he was in but couldn't help him.

After some time, I asked the other boys about Mark. They said Mark had not been to Rehab, that he had only dropped out of high school a few months ago, and that he had a family at home who loved him. They said his mother was working selling items near the bridge every evening and that we should talk to her. I confronted Mark about his lies and asked him what was really going on. He didn't really tell me and continued to insist that he had been to Rehab before. I still had difficulties with the language barrier, and even with translation found it difficult. Mark knew this and deliberately left things vague. Mark was in his final year of high school when he dropped out, so his English was pretty good, but he kept this quiet. I could tell that he understood a lot of what we, as crew members, were saying to each other and he used this for his own advantage at times.

I kept trying to persuade Mark to go back to school and re-enroll for the year. As it was September, he had only missed a few months. I knew his teachers would give him a chance if he asked them. He kept agreeing to this and then changing his mind at the last minute. I got really frustrated with him, but eventually he agreed to re-enroll the following Monday.

Luke also told us that his family was thinking of moving to Manila so that he would be able to go to school. He said they might be leaving at any time. We had promised all of the boys that they could visit the ship before we left, so we took Mark and Luke for an initial visit. The other boys were not happy, but we justified it on the basis that the two of them would be going to school soon and may not have another chance to visit the ship. They got really upset, accusing me of favouritism, but eventually they sent Joel as a representative to question me. When I explained it carefully to him, he said "Okay" and pulled the other boys away. It was hard to leave them all behind at the gate, but we didn't have the capacity to take them all on the ship at this stage, especially when they had been inhaling solvents.

When we arrived on the ship, all of the crew were really friendly as they had heard a lot about the boys. I introduced them to some of the crew members who already knew their names as they had seen pictures. They were walking around as if they were royalty and Luke kept going up to everyone and loudly saying "Hi!" and waving at them. It was pretty funny. Then we went into the Book Fair and they were fascinated by the books. They both sat on the floor in the hobbies section, pulled books off the shelves about all sorts of subjects, and just sat there looking at the pictures. It occurred to me that maybe they didn't have the chance to look at books normally, and this made me sad. In the West, we take having access to good books and reading material for granted.

After they were finished with the books, we took them for a tour of the ship and they especially enjoyed having photos taken wearing the Captain's hat on the bridge (control centre) of the ship. They had juice in the dining room and then it was time to leave. Mark indicated that he was cold so one of the crew gave him her jumper. Luke also wanted one so I gave him one of mine but then he was complaining loudly because it didn't have a hood! Later, all of this clothing was either sold or swapped amongst the boys anyway. The only boy who didn't sell things was Matthew (the leader) and he accumulated a large number of our items. We took the two boys back to the bridge area after their visit and then went back to the ship.

Over time, I became close to Mark as I wanted to get to the root of his troubles and try to help him. I especially wanted to see him back in school. He told us one day that he didn't want to stay on the street with the others that evening. He was worried about their influence as he was trying to stay clear of the solvents. So we took him with us to the ship, but this caused a massive problem with the other boys who suddenly appeared in a group as we were leaving and started running around us shouting. They even broke through the barrier past the security and tried to follow us but the security guards stopped them and I was forced to tell them that we were only taking Mark with us.

When they protested, I told them it was because they had been inhaling solvents and I could smell it on them. We started a practice of getting them to breathe so that we could smell if they were high or not. The other boys were really angry, apart from a boy called Paul who didn't even bother to breathe to try and prove that he wasn't high. He knew that he was high already and that our decision was fair. Fairness was very important to the boys and we were careful to observe this. Mark pulled a face at the others as we walked off, which I wasn't happy about as he was deliberately taunting them. Later, we heard that Mark too was taking drugs every day and that he was deceiving us, but street boys don't generally tell tales about each other so we weren't aware at the time.

During Mark's second visit to the ship, he wanted to play a game of chess. Mark beat me which I was surprised about! I'm not great at chess, but I know how to play and he was a street kid who was damaging his brain by inhaling solvents every day! Mark then mentioned that he had been a chess champion at his school. I told him again that he must make sure he went back to school that week and that I would be coming with him to see his tutor. He also agreed to go back to his house and live there with his family.

After the ship visit, we took Mark back to Olongapo and went to meet his mum who was selling food in the city. His mum was really nice and didn't understand why Mark was on the street. She said he had his own room at home and enough food to eat. She mentioned that initially it had been a problem with a girlfriend that had started the issue. Mark said that he would go home with his mum and stay there.

However, we soon found that we were going round in circles with Mark. The following day, when we came to set up the book table on the bridge, he was sleeping there alone. Usually there were various boys sleeping on the bridge in a huddle waiting for us to arrive in the morning. We woke them up when we arrived for ministry. But this time Mark was there alone. I woke him up and asked him why he was there and what had happened. His clothes were really very dirty in comparison to the other boys, who somehow kept themselves relatively clean. Mark said there were problems at his house. When we pushed him, for more information, he said that his older brother often beat him up when drunk. So I went with Mark later that day to talk to his mum and brother about the problems and try to resolve them so he could go home. His mum said that actually there was no problem and his brother told us that they just wanted Mark back home.

We repeated this scenario every day with Mark, arriving to find him asleep on the bridge after having promised us that he would go home the day before. Many times I sat on the floor with him on arrival and talked to him about his life. At times he covered his ears and said, "No English, no English," pretending not to understand, but I knew he just didn't want to hear what I had to say. It was at this time that a local woman walked past and said to me, "They're rugby boys, don't you know?" as if it was a secret and as if I would say, "Oh my goodness, yes you're right. I must get away from them at once." I just said, "I love them and Jesus does too." But her comment summed up local attitudes even amongst some of the Christians. It was as if these "rugby boys" were some sort of alien species that had invaded. I heard many similar comments, but this one stuck in my mind as a good representation.

I couldn't find evidence that Mark was taking drugs, but the other boys were so upset with him that they broke their golden rule to tell us that he was. I knew that there was something in this because there was a big division in the group. Mark was on one side and all of the other boys on the other and they were leaving him to sleep alone. I thought it was because the other boys were inhaling solvents and he wasn't, but I wasn't sure if he was deceiving us since he had lied before. I really couldn't understand what was going on, and got more and more frustrated with Mark.

The day before we were due to go to Mark's school, I made him promise again that he would go home, have a shower, and change into clean clothes so that he looked presentable at his school. When we arrived at the bridge, in the morning, he was there again asleep, but at least he had changed his clothes and looked cleaner. We went to his school and a teacher lectured us for an hour about the pitfalls of dropping out of school and missing classes before we convinced him to allow Mark to re-enroll. The teacher said we needed to speak to Mark's specific tutor for her to arrange a special test for him to catch up. Mark's tutor said that he was a good student and that he had been chess champion at the school the previous year and had won a lot of money for the school in a tournament in Manila. She said to Mark, "What's happened to you? You used to be handsome!" She was talking about his massive weight-loss and general state of unhealthiness due to drug addiction. She was kind and agreed to the special test to re-enroll him. The date for the test was arranged.

Shortly after this, I was walking in the city in the evening with Arlene. As we approached the bridge leading back to the ship, I saw a lone figure standing in the shadows watching the people walking past. He was unsteady on his feet and rocking backwards and forwards holding a plastic bag in his hand. As I moved nearer, I saw it was Mark. He ran away when he saw me and tried to hide but didn't get very far and so he sat on the ground, behind a large pillar, in the shadows, breathing heavily. I sat beside him on the ground, which was dirty and really stank, and when I put my arm around his shoulders I smelt the intoxicatingly strong smell of the solvent.

The boys had recently stopped taking "rugby" and had moved on to a door sealant called "Vuca Seal" which was stronger. It was all over him and he reeked of it. I covered my nose. I remember this was the only time where the thought ran through my mind that I could see how addiction to this smell was created because it was really intoxicating. I knew I needed to be careful not to breathe much of it in, but Mark was really very high. He was vacant and staring ahead, and then he began crying again as I tried to talk to him. I asked him why he was doing this to himself and what was it that had made him so unhappy, but he didn't answer.

Arlene went to get Mark's mum who was working nearby because I didn't know what to do and I didn't want to leave him alone and miserable. His mum got very upset and begged him to come home. Mark got up when she arrived and stumbled away as we all watched him go. I followed and tried to talk to him again, sharing a bit of my life before I became a Christian and how miserable I had been. His hopelessness reminded me of my old life when I was immersed in drink, gambling and meaningless relationships. I knew Mark was listening as I shared the hope that I had found with him, but he didn't respond. Eventually, we had to leave him, alone and staring vacantly ahead of himself hanging over a railing. I was really worried that he wouldn't make it through the night if he inhaled any more solvents, but he didn't seem to care and our attention and concern was only making things worse.

After this, we experienced serious problems with Mark at the bridge. Sometimes I wasn't even aware that he was there, but then I would catch a glimpse of him standing at a distance staring at us. I knew he had been abusing solvents, even though he always denied it, so I walked over to him but he ran away. I chased after him and he shouted, "No, Ma'am Natalie, no." as he tried to hide under some cardboard, because he didn't want me to smell the drugs on him. The smell was very strong and I told him that he wouldn't be able to go back to school if he couldn't sort out his addiction. But he was playing games with us, encouraging the other boys to take solvents with no intention of stopping himself. His behaviour only got worse.

16: Paul: A Special Friendship

One special story is that of Paul (14.) Paul wasn't around that much at the beginning of our ministry. He was taller than the other boys and seemed tougher in many ways. He had obviously been on the street for a long time and was missing all of his front teeth. In a small way, to look at him reminded me of my brother James who died in a car accident in 2002. But that was where the similarity ended. Paul was rude and obnoxious. He made it clear that he didn't appreciate us being there and didn't like us. He didn't like the influence we were having on the younger boys. He took what he could get from us and left. He was obviously using us.

Despite this, we tried to treat all the boys as equals, so as not to create problems with allegations of favouritism. Several times, when Paul arrived, I tried to talk to him but he rudely ignored me or began talking to one of the other boys as if he hadn't heard me. He deliberately annoyed me by sitting in the way or just generally being a nuisance. He rarely smiled and would hold his hand out to make demands and say, "Give me!" all of the time. On one occasion, he became irritated and angry with one of the younger boys and kicked him hard in the ribs. I was shocked as I hadn't seen such violence amongst the boys.

However, I saw at other times, that Paul was generous with the other boys and shared his food with the younger boys even though he didn't have much himself. I realised that he had become accustomed to fighting for survival after many years on the street. Although Paul was a tall boy he was very thin and underweight. He came to our table but then just lazed around sleeping underneath it or on a chair nearby. I noticed that he started to come more frequently but he still wouldn't really address us or pay any attention to us. Sometimes he took the guitar and started singing out of tune in a language nobody really understood which he described as "street language."   I was joking around with some boys, one day, and placed one of their arms around Paul. He got really mad and loudly said, "No!" He grabbed my arm, and demonstrated what I had done, and made it clear he didn't like it. I got the message. He also told one of the other boys off when they were cuddling me saying, "You are fifteen years old, not a baby."

Over time, I began to like this boy. Some of the ladies selling things regularly on the bridge asked him to man their stalls whilst they went to get drinks. He was trustworthy and never tried to take anything. Once I saw Reuben, one of the younger boys, approaching an old beggar man who was sound asleep on the bridge. He picked up his begging pot, tipped the money out into his hand, put the empty pot back, and sauntered off casually grinning as he walked past us. Paul looked at me as I tried to process what I had just witnessed, he saw that I was shocked and didn't know what to do about this blatant thieving. Paul grinned but confronted Reuben and without needing to say anything, held his hand out for the money. Reuben automatically gave it to him due to the age hierarchy of authority amongst the boys. Paul then woke the man up gently by tapping him and gave the money back. Paul began appearing at the bridge, every day, with or without the other boys. He didn't say hello but held up his hand for a high five; then he sat down and hung around for most of the day.

A local Pastor that came to the bridge said that he knew Paul and that he had been following him around the city for at least a year trying to give him food. When the Pastor first arrived, Paul was lying on the ground and he acknowledged the Pastor. The Pastor told him to sit up and he obeyed, grinning to himself. I noted that he did have some respect for authority. Paul confirmed through the Pastor that he really didn't like us when we first arrived on the bridge but when we asked for a reason he said that he didn't know why. The Pastor told us later that Paul was one of the worst street boys and the most difficult to handle, a fact we were already aware of.

Over time, the barriers came down and I saw that Paul was warming to us, although he never would have admitted it. One day, we were having a conversation whilst he was lying in his favourite position, on the ground underneath the table. During the conversation, he pointed his fingers at me indicating a gun. I laughed at him and said, "Why do you want to kill me?" I thought he would say "Yes" or "I already have" or something, but he said "No" very definitely and watched to see my reaction. So I asked him "Why?" and he said "Because you are good." I was caught off guard by this assertion from a boy like Paul with real attitude. It struck me that he wasn't messing around and that he had taken some time to come to this conclusion. I gathered my thoughts and said: "Only because of Jesus." And he nodded to acknowledge this. We had this same conversation several times after that and it became a bit of a joke, but I will always remember that first time being caught off guard and realising that we were having an impact on these boys, albeit slowly.

Paul often asked to borrow my MP3 player and listened to the music or watched the music videos for hours. The boys always found the video of me and some others from the ship singing "Kay Buti Buti Mo Panginoon" (The Lord is good) on the MP3 player and played it loudly singing along. The younger boys also borrowed my camera sometimes and took many pictures of themselves posing. I kept an eye on the location of these items when they were using them, but there was a time when I wasn't paying enough attention and Paul wandered off with my MP3 player. I waited for a while, convinced he would come back, but then started to worry, not really about the item but about what I would do if he didn't return. Local people saw that I was looking around and they had seen him leave. One man said, "That's the last you'll see of that. You'd better go to the police." And other people expressed similar thoughts. But I said, "He will come back." After ten or fifteen minutes, Paul sauntered back casually carrying the MP3 player and some rice that he was eating, as if nothing was wrong. I was relieved and just said to him, "Please stay here if you have this" and he nodded. I could see from his nonchalant expression that he was testing me to see if I trusted him or trying to prove that he was trustworthy.

Really Paul was testing us to see if we practiced what we were preaching. I liked him as his loyalty was harder to gain and therefore worth more. Some of the other boys were quite superficial in their loyalties, as evidenced by the thefts and other problems. But once we had gained Paul's trust, we didn't lose it. His background was quite confusing, but we established that he had been on and off the street since he was 7 and had spent a year in Rehab at 12. To start with, he wasn't really interested in changing his life and spoke about wanting to "still go around" the city. Over time, this changed and I believed that he might really be serious about wanting to leave the street.

Then one of the older boys told me that Paul was very ill and had been vomiting blood. He said there had been an X Ray which showed a hole in Paul's lung and that it was really serious. I was very upset as I was close to him by this point. Later that day, I was coming out of the mall, with my "Halo halo," (a mixture of all types of food including beans, sweetcorn, jelly, milk and ice-cream and a dessert delicacy in the Philippines!) which I bought for lunch every day, and I saw Paul standing at the entrance. He was leaning inside the door but he knew that he wasn't allowed to go in as the security guards would stop him. He wasn't focusing on me as I was coming towards him because he was obviously high on solvents, but as I got nearer he saw me and acknowledged me. He then put my arm around his neck, a practice the older boys adopted as a more manly sign of affection than the younger ones cuddles.

We walked together back towards the bridge and I decided to broach the subject of his illness with him. I had already determined to make him go to the hospital but knew I had to handle it carefully as he might refuse if I put pressure on him. I said, "I hear that you are ill and have been coughing blood." He just nodded. I told him that it made me sad as I didn't want something bad to happen to him. I asked him if he would come to the hospital with me. He didn't want to go, but when we got back to the bridge he pointed at my "Halo halo" and asked me to give it to him. This was my lunch every day and I never gave it away, the boys knew this and didn't ask me for it. In fact, if a new boy who didn't know the rules came and asked me for my "halo halo" the other boys told him off and said it was my lunch.

On this day, I was so upset about Paul's illness that I gave it to him. His eyes brightened and he seemed surprised as he wasn't really expecting me to give it to him. He then got the spoon and started feeding all of the other younger boys with bits from it before having any himself. It was quite a sight as they all sat on the floor waiting to be fed with a spoon, even though they were eleven and twelve years old. I then asked him again about the hospital and later, with the help of his friends, persuaded him to go. He agreed, but only if Mark accompanied him.

At the hospital, I decided it was time that he really understood the Gospel. I really wasn't sure if he had been listening before and I wasn't sure how ill he really was. Arlene translated the discussion. The first things we established were that he thought it would make him a better person if he went to church. He said this with such sincerity and I could see that he really thought he was a terrible person in the sight of God. He then said that he couldn't go into church because he didn't know how to pray and that he couldn't pray as he was too dirty. Later I kept thinking about Paul's sincere (but wrong) beliefs about God and I wondered how many others felt like this. Here we are in the West arrogantly ignoring God and acting as if he doesn't exist, but Paul didn't dare to approach God, thinking he would be rejected. I explained the truth to Paul, and when I told him how Jesus died on the cross for his sin, he immediately said that he knew about this already because I had taught it to them on the bridge, which was encouraging.

When we went in to see the Doctor, Paul and Mark both had tests and X Rays. They weren't very well behaved and kept messing around with equipment, leaving and going outside and wandering around. When the Nurse couldn't find Paul's pulse the two boys thought this was hilarious and Paul grabbed his heart and acted as if he was about to keel over and die. I was unhappy with the Doctor's attitude as she looked at the boys with distaste throughout the proceedings, and spoke about them as if they weren't there, when giving their results.

Mark's X-ray was completely clear, again evidencing his lack of long term drug abuse. Paul's X-ray showed deep scar tissue on his lung and the Doctor told us he had Tuberculosis (TB.) I asked her if it was advanced and she said yes. She didn't show any compassion or any love towards him at all. I was left to ask the questions about what would happen and, not really knowing anything about the disease, I was really concerned. She gave us a prescription for Paul and we left. Paul and Mark were joking around, but I knew it had to be false bravado on Paul's part as this was serious. I was annoyed with Mark for making it so trivial, but realised that his immaturity meant that he didn't know any better.

 It also hit me that TB is very contagious and that Paul often shared his food with the other boys, and was even eating from the same spoon. I too had not really taken extra precautions with the boys, but I was less worried about that as I had been vaccinated and was always careful not to eat from or drink from the same things as them, which is the main way the disease is spread. I told him that he mustn't now share his food, but it took a while for him to remember this as this had always been his practice. To start with I reminded him, but on occasions I forgot and one day I even encouraged him to share with another boy. He looked surprised and I thought he was being less than generous until he gave the water to the other boy and then said to me, "But I'm sick." I tried to stop the other boy from drinking it, but it was too late. As far as I'm aware, none of the others caught TB from Paul.

In any event, after leaving the hospital we went to a pharmacy to buy Paul's medicine. I looked him in the eyes and told him that whilst taking the medicine he mustn't take any drugs or it could kill him. He promised me but then said, "But I will be hungry." I responded, "Right, if that's the reason I promise you that I will make sure you have enough food every day until the ship leaves."

To prove we were serious about this, we took Paul and Mark to a restaurant and said they could order what they wanted. They both ate a lot and asked for more rice. Later Arlene and Mark were outside and I was left with Paul who was finishing his rice. He looked at me and said seriously, "Ma'am Natalie, thank you for trying to help us." I nodded, but had to look away because the tears came again. Here was a hardened street boy saying thank you, maybe for the first time in many years. He finished his rice and put his thumb up to indicate that he had enjoyed it. When we got outside they both said they were full so we went back to the ship, leaving them to go and find somewhere to sleep.

17: Loss of Control

The next day Paul was very quiet and there was a problem between him and Mark. I knew immediately what it was, so I asked Paul, "Did Mark try and get you to take drugs with him last night, and now he is mad because you refused?" He didn't say anything at first, but I persisted and eventually he nodded. There was an ongoing conflict for Paul after this as he tried to keep his loyalties to his friends and also to us at the same time.

My promise to ensure Paul had proper food everyday brought its own problems. Some might describe this promise as unwise or rash, but I knew that if necessary I could arrange for funds to be transferred from my personal account in England so it wasn't an empty promise. The problem really was how best to fulfil it. The issue of what to do when someone asked me for food was (and still is) a constant battle because I found myself thinking, "Who am I to decide whether this person eats or not today?" Knowing that I had the financial capability to buy food for them most of the time meant that I often relented, unless I could see that it would do more harm than good, for example, professional beggars. But I had to balance this with the knowledge that I couldn't feed everyone. Mostly I just settled for buying food for people that specifically asked for it or offering food instead of money to those asking for the latter.

We realised straight away that we needed to begin some kind of feeding programme, but didn't really know where to start or who to ask. We asked the ship leadership but they said they didn't have the budget for it, and we had already been advised earlier in the ministry that we mustn't allow the ministry with the boys to turn into anything long term. I knew when I made the promise to Paul that we couldn't just feed him. We would need to feed all of our regular boys. We borrowed and begged money from crew members on the ship who gave generously to help us. Most crew members knew of our work on the bridge as they saw us when visiting the city and I had asked for prayer several times at the weekly prayer meeting. Also, every time any of the 400 crew members went into the city the boys asked them, "Where is Ma'am Natalie?" and told them that I was their "friend."

So to begin with, whilst we were trying to establish something more official through local churches, we took the boys twice a day to various street food stands and bought them all food. Unfortunately, this caused fights everyday as the boys argued about who could have which item and complained that one of them had more than another. Also, other boys that we didn't know would try and join the group to get food and inevitably there were tears when things went wrong.

On one really bad day, Paul had been asking me all day if we could take them to a particular place to eat as there were only four of them. I said it would be ok if no more boys appeared, but by the end of the day there were more than seven of them, so I told him we were just going to our normal stand as it was cheaper. Paul got really upset and angry. Then he sat on the ground and refused to eat. Some of the other boys also joined him and refused even to look at me or talk to me. Mark took the lead in the rebellion as usual. Suddenly he turned to me and said in a voice thick with hatred, "Me, no back to school, no back to school."

This was one of the only occasions when I totally lost my temper with them. Mark's comments, after all the effort I had made in getting him re-enrolled, really made me angry. I knew he had been waiting for this chance to rebel as he wasn't really interested in going back to school yet and that he wouldn't change his mind having made this statement. I shouted at them that they were ungrateful and I told Mark that I didn't care whether he went back to school or not. As far as I was concerned if he threw away his life it was his business and I really didn't care anymore as I'd had enough. I was really upset, so we left. Arlene went back after a few minutes to buy the food for Paul that he had requested. I felt guilty as I knew he was dealing with his illness and it was Mark that had really made me angry.

The next day, when we arrived at the bridge, the boys were all sleeping there as usual, so I went straight over to Paul and apologised if I had upset him the day before. He accepted this immediately and although things were a bit strained at first, as it was the first time the boys had seen me lose my temper and they were shocked, they returned to normal after a while. I realised that Paul had believed that I had broken my promise about the food and, as was often the case, the language barrier had caused the confusion.

18: Local Churches: Please Help Us!

At this time we approached several churches in the area to ask for help with a basic feeding programme. The idea was that it would just be a temporary programme for up to ten boys and that, as most of the boys had now made decisions to leave the street, the programme would only continue until we had found them new places to live.

Unfortunately, the local churches didn't really understand our situation. They were all keen to help when we said we were from Logos Hope, but as soon as we mentioned who we were working with and what we needed help with, they backed away. Again it was as if being a "rugby boy" made them somehow less human. We received responses including, "Our members don't really know how to deal with that kind of boy" and, " Here's a few hundred pesos" and, " We will need all sorts of paperwork, a detailed plan of your goals and objectives" etc. One church, that did have a heart for the ministry, was already involved in so many other ministries, that they were unable to really get involved in helping us, although they did try. It was pretty frustrating but we realised we would have to go it alone for now. Local people often approached us on the bridge to tell us how kind we were and to thank us for caring for their street children, but most were unwilling to be involved themselves.

I realised that even Christian's didn't know how to help these boys, had other priorities, or were unwilling. In many cases, I think people wanted to help but were afraid that their help wouldn't be appreciated or that they might get attacked or rejected in some way. In most cases, the boys had become invisible to people as they were so used to seeing them under the bridge inhaling solvents. It was now normal, and people didn't think beyond this to the damage that the solvents were doing and that they were just children. A new believer friend of mine in the UK, when speaking about evangelism, recently said to me, "If you see someone standing in front of a car about to get run over, you pull them out of the way, right?" His faith was so new and the Gospel had hit home so powerfully, without any of the confusion that blinds us over time, that he could see the reality for all people. It is the same with these boys; they are killing themselves gradually day by day and Christians are just ignoring them for a number of reasons.

One local church was very helpful to us in many ways, such as allowing us to store our equipment from the bridge in their building every day. We were really grateful, and sometimes the members spoke of joining us at the bridge, but nobody came for more than a few minutes at a time in the end. I mention the next incidents, not as a criticism of this individual church because I believe this is a representation of how many local churches and church members would behave. I hope readers will use these experiences to educate and inform Christians and Churches, so that they can adapt not just to tolerate these children, but to really love and care for them as well. I really hope not to offend or upset any individuals by detailing the next few incidents, but I think it is necessary to highlight the type of behaviour that can alienate, reject or upset a street child who has already experienced these things in abundance.

The sad thing was that the boys accompanied us into this church every day, as they helped us carry boxes and tables and other things, but the members didn't take the opportunities to engage with them. The boys occasionally took a shower in the restroom area of the church, not by invitation but by locking themselves in the bathroom and stripping off before we realised what was going on. I was worried about the water everywhere afterwards, but the church leaders were okay about this. But at other times, people withdrew and ignored them when the boys came into the church. I was desperate to get these boys introduced in a church and was so disappointed by this missed opportunity.

One day, Mark and Reuben came in with us and the church youth were doing a craft activity together in a group at tables. Mark was standing at a distance and staring at the activity. I could tell he would have loved to have joined in, but there was an invisible wall, a barrier that I could see and I'm sure Mark could too. It was like he was looking into a house from outside and wasn't allowed in. Just watching him made my eyes fill with tears for the hundred millionth time as I said, "Come on, let's go." Then I put my arm around his shoulders and led him away.

Another time, Reuben picked up a leaflet advertising a youth event, but a church member quickly took it away from him whilst muttering something, and I could tell that they wouldn't be welcome to attend. The church members and leadership were very polite and helpful to us as foreigners and members of the Logos Hope, but what about their own Filipino children right on their doorstep? Someone needed to take responsibility and help these boys. Why not the Church? What would Jesus do?

19: Feeding Programme

We gave up approaching churches after a while and happened to meet a ship volunteer named Zee on the way back to the ship one evening. (Crew members serve on the ship for one or two years at a time and travel to the ship from countries all around the world. Generally the ship volunteers are local people that join the ship in a particular port and remain on-board for the duration of the port, maybe for three or four weeks.) Myself and Arlene were discussing our desire for a temporary feeding ministry to try and give the boys the chance to come off the solvents. We spoke about how desperate we were for someone to help us as we had been working with these boys for so long and had really built strong relationships with them.

Zee offered us an immediate solution which sounded too good to be true. Her family was renting a business premise in the city with a large room on the ground floor that was suitable for providing food for the boys every day. Its primary purpose was as a shop but the family lived in the rooms upstairs. There was also a pool table in the room, which could be used with supervision. This was the kind of offer we had been desperately waiting and praying for. We worked out a plan to provide two meals a day on a temporary basis. We obtained donations from our ship friends to pay for the food. We were just so grateful for this suggestion and the willingness that accompanied it. The Book Fair Manager's face was a picture when I mentioned this to him, as he was already very worried that the ministry was becoming too large for us to handle, but he allowed us to go ahead on the basis that we were funding the project ourselves and that it would be temporary. Little did we know that we were about to open a huge can of worms!

Zee also told us about a Christian couple who had been volunteering on the ship who had previously taken in boys from problem families. She told us that this was their ministry and that they might be willing to consider taking in some of our boys. We didn't realise that the couple hadn't taken street boys before. We asked her to put us in touch with them as soon as possible. I was having trouble sleeping, as each boy and what to do with him was going around and around in my head all of the time, especially as the ship's time in Subic Bay had to be drawing to a close, or so I thought. We had a core group of only nine or ten boys left at that time, as many of the older boys were working and some of the younger ones had gone home or back to school.

We went to visit the premises for the proposed feeding programme and couldn't quite believe it. It was enormous with a large long table in the centre and the promised pool table in a separate area. It was really perfect for our purposes. We were introduced to Zee's family who were willing to fit the cooking and supervision of the feeding ministry around their business activities. I don't think any of us really knew what we were letting ourselves in for, but we were all willing to give it a shot.

We started straight away by inviting the boys to come and have lunch with us from the bridge. They were intrigued and followed us in a line through the city, not knowing what to expect. It took twenty minutes to locate them all and get them ready. They seemed a bit dazed and confused at first, but they followed us nevertheless. On arrival, the excited chatter diminished as we walked up the steps outside and rang the doorbell. We walked inside and into the big hall and there was the table already laid with dishes and utensils. There was utter and complete silence as the boys walked in and looked around. They really didn't know what to make of all this and were totally overwhelmed. They just stood near to the table not knowing what to do, until the father of the family told them to go and wash their hands in the bathroom and prepare to eat. Without a word, they proceeded single file to the bathroom to do as they were told. The silence continued for another ten minutes or so as the food was dished up and we prayed and began to eat. They were in complete shock and were very polite and well behaved. Gradually, the normal chatter returned, which was a relief as it was strange to see them so quiet and subdued.

After eating, they were allowed to stay for a little while and use the pool table. They were also allowed to take a shower in the bathroom area. Then we said we would collect them later as they were to come back at 6pm for another meal. I noted that Paul was the only one who appeared not to have taken solvents during this day. We had started the feeding programme because of his medical diagnosis, but really it was something we had wanted to do for a while. Later, we talked about how the first day had gone. The boys all returned at 6pm as planned and everything went smoothly. They were very polite throughout the day and expressed their thanks to the family and to us. The family developed a relationship with the boys straight away which was great to see and something that I hadn't anticipated would happen when we set the ministry in motion.

During one of the sessions, I became aware that my eating habits were a fascination to the boys. They watched me eat with concern and asked frequently why I was eating the chicken before the rice. I explained that, if a person is not used to eating rice, their body needs to adjust to it gradually, but they couldn't understand this and saw it as most irregular and strange. Reuben watched me carefully and one day jumped up from his seat at the table before rushing around to my seat. He grabbed my spoon and fork from me, swapped them around, and exclaimed, "No no no, Ma'am Natalie," I swapped back when he wasn't looking, but it was no good because he always noticed and repeated the whole thing again. This left me, and everyone else, in fits of laughter, as it brought back memories of primary school and being shouted at for eating with my knife and fork the wrong way around.

The team discussed how we were going to take this ministry forward. The boys said they inhaled solvents because they were hungry. We knew that this was part of the reason, but we suspected this was not the whole truth. We decided to put this assertion to the test. This wasn't a game or an experiment with the children. Our ultimate goal was to see if the boys could come off the solvents by providing them with enough food, thus encouraging them to think about their lives and futures. We were also conscious that it was unfair to boys like Paul, who were making a real attempt to come off the drugs, if we forced them into an environment where they were mixing with others who had taken drugs due to the smell that emanated from the culprits.

So, we told the boys in advance that they would only be allowed into the building for their lunch and dinner if they hadn't taken any solvents during that day. We tested their truthfulness by smelling them, a practice we had already adopted on previous occasions.

Some of the boys tried to get around this by making an exhaling sound without breathing any air out, but generally we could tell. Unfortunately, this turned our peaceful gatherings into a war.

20: Teething Problems

On the first day, only two boys, Paul and Adam, were allowed in and we turned the others away at the door. Paul had been solvent free for a while now, and was counting the days. He was becoming more energetic as he came off the solvents and more willing to stand against the others. Adam had been somewhere else for the day so he hadn't spent time with the others and therefore hadn't taken any drugs. We saw the massive influence the group mentality and peer pressure was having on them all. The excluded boys didn't accept their fate. At first, they stood silently outside, but then the insults began. They shouted personal things at me, accusing me of favouritism. They cursed and swore until they were told off by Zee's father, who was not impressed. The worst thing was that the gate at the entrance to the premises was made of metal bars with gaps, so they watched us eating from the doorway for the whole meal, which made us and the other boys feel really bad. But we knew we had to stick to our rules.

After the first few days, the boys knew that we meant what we said, and most of the time they didn't show up if they had taken solvents. Mark was the only one who sometimes made the deliberate decision to take drugs rather than eat and he was still having a negative influence on the others. When he did attend, it was noted that his clothes were so dirty that they left a mark on his chair. I still didn't know what had happened to him to make him so indifferent to his life. We had a few problems with Reuben also refusing to do as he was told, and to stop playing pool when he was meant to, but things were generally peaceful.

There were several days when I caught the boys red-handed, inhaling solvents in the daytime before we were due for the evening meal. Once, in the market area, I walked up behind them and could tell they were high. They denied it, but then I smelt them and confirmed it, so I told them not to bother coming to the meal. Reuben was one of the boys I was closest to at this time and I was especially sad to see him abusing solvents, but unfortunately he didn't seem to have the will to take a stand, and was often excluded from our meals. Whenever we excluded them, the boys got really angry and upset, as if we hadn't given them fair warning.

One day I was travelling in a Jeepney when I saw a group of them in the street on the opposite side of the road to the feeding ministry venue blatantly inhaling solvents. I couldn't believe that they would do this right outside the feeding premises, so I jumped out of the Jeepney and confronted them. They looked really guilty and tried to hide the evidence, but it was too late. I excluded them from the evening meal. Luke gave me the remainder of his drugs in the plastic bag and told me to throw it on the roof. They walked down the road with me trying to persuade me to change my mind. I hated to exclude them but I had to be firm for the sake of the other boys, so I refused. They followed me, calling me names and using bad words, which really upset me.

Our principle was to start again every day and give them another chance, no matter what they had done the day before. So they said sorry and we said it was okay and tried to forget that any really hurtful behaviour had happened. The boys were so bad at times that they were apologising every day, and sometimes for really bad and hurtful behaviour. They started saying, "Really, it's okay?" and, "Why do you always forgive us?" This was a great opportunity to tell them that we forgave them for their sin against us because Jesus had forgiven us for our sins against Him. This was much more effective than just telling them that this is how Christians should behave; they could really see it and see that we loved them despite the way they treated us at times.

I made a big mistake one day due to not being flexible enough. In my mind, we were trying to help a specific group of nine or ten boys. This is the number that we were paying to feed and the number that we had been working with for some time. These were the boys that we knew well and wanted to see leaving the street for better lives.

The problem was that sometimes there would be an extra boy or two appearing, having slept with the others overnight for a variety of reasons, usually relating to problems at home. The dilemma for me was what to do with these boys. I envisioned a nightmare scenario where, instead of the feeding ministry becoming smaller and therefore less expensive as we re-housed these boys, it just got larger and larger as we picked up the boys on the fringes. I knew that many of these other boys didn't have enough to eat at home and we didn't want to advertise our feeding programme widely, as we just didn't have the funding to continue it long term. We were relying on donations from crew members with no other funding. The food was costing around 1200 pesos (£17) a day. It was meant to be a temporary solution, providing somewhere for the boys to come off solvents and to go from there to a new home environment. We did see massive changes in the boys after only a few days, as they came out of their drug-induced haze and started thinking about their lives and their futures. They came back to life and there were a lot more smiles and energy.

The worst thing about this situation was that I would have loved to have taken all of the extra boys in and helped them as well, but we just didn't have the capacity, so we had to say no. On this day, an additional boy named Jonah was with the other boys and he obviously wanted to eat with us. We said no, but the other boys protested, telling us that his dad had been recently murdered or had murdered someone, I can't remember which, as we often heard stories like this! The other boys said that they would share their food with him. I should've agreed to this as it was fairly reasonable, but I felt I had to stick to my guns to stop them inviting all of their friends. This caused a big problem for some of the boys who thought I was being cruel to exclude one boy.

We went and ate, but the atmosphere was sad as Jonah was sitting outside. His friend inside, Joel, developed an attitude and was determined that he would get his way. I automatically reacted against this as he tried to get around me when I had already said no. He said he was going to give his food to Jonah outside. I told him not to, but he was really insistent, and eventually I lost my temper with him. I shouted at him that it was our money and that we were paying for them as individuals to eat, that they should be grateful and not start putting conditions or demands on us, and that we decided who to invite.

Joel stood up and shouted, "Why didn't you tell us that you were paying for this?" I left the table and went outside, as I was really upset and frustrated. Jonah was sitting outside, not really knowing what to do. I felt really bad that we had excluded him. A few of the boys came out and sat with me as I was upset, but Joel was still angry, asking me why I had spoken about money and saying that if we didn't want to do it for them then we shouldn't do it. He said that it made them feel guilty when we spoke about money.

Then things got worse as Matthew (the leader) appeared, obviously having been summoned by someone because of the problem. He saw that I was upset and shouted at Jonah in an attempt to defend me saying, "What's the problem here? Are you causing problems?" and hit him hard on the back. I really felt bad now as this poor kid hadn't had any food and was now being assaulted by an older boy on my behalf! I tried to calm things down and to explain to the boys that I was really just trying to help them, but I got frustrated when they were ungrateful. The following day I apologised to Joel for shouting at him and he accepted this, but our relationship was difficult from then on.

After this incident, we allowed a few extra boys to come, providing they shared the food of our regular boys and that they didn't invite extra people on purpose. We didn't have any further problems in this respect. One of the extra boys, John, turned up on the bridge occasionally, and because I had never seen him before I thought he was new. His English was pretty good, and I could tell he was going to school. He seemed to know the other boys a bit, but I didn't think he was one of them. So when he came up from under the bridge really high one day and fell asleep on the ground near our table, I looked after him and was really worried about him, believing it was his first time inhaling solvents. When he woke up, I gave him a big lecture about drugs, and I also lectured the other boys about getting new people involved, and being a bad influence, etc. I later found out that this boy had already been to Rehab for one year and was clearly one of them already. I felt pretty stupid.

Mark continued to cause problems, and one day we had gathered the whole group for the evening meal. Mark was in a bad mood and was arguing and demanding things straight away. We went via a clothes shop to buy some new shorts for Reuben, as they had indecent holes in them. Whilst in the shop, Mark deliberately kept trying to attack Adam, a younger boy. He crouched on the ground like a karate expert and I was afraid, as I knew Mark could really hurt Adam. We tried to stay in-between the two of them, but Mark was intent on having a fight and moved around, trying to take swipes at Adam. I got really angry with him, as he was one of the older boys that we were closer to, and he should've known better.

Outside, Mark stormed off up the street and refused to come back. We let him go, glad to be rid of him, until he returned with alcohol and tried to get the others to drink it. We went straight to the feeding venue, and banned him from entering unless he ditched the alcohol, which he did. But these types of incidents with Mark were becoming more frequent, and I still didn't understand him. No amount of reasoning changed his mind if he had decided on a course of action, and he was a really bad influence on the other boys.

We had problems on most days now, as we continued to divide the group. We encouraged those who really wanted to change to leave their street family behind and take the opportunity being offered to them. The problem was that, because I was the closest to most of them and had spent the most time with them, when they were upset or angry they always targeted me. This targeting was inevitably personal, as they knew by now how to upset me. This even continued on Facebook when I was on the ship in the evenings. My support at several stages came from an unlikely source. Paul started defending me, asking Reuben, "Why do you always get mad with Ma'am Natalie?" He also became angry with Simon and told him not to say anything else about me. I think he was fed up with the younger ones complaining and being ungrateful. It was hard for him to do this, but his loyalties were changing, and I began to have hope for his future.

21: The Worst Day

The worst day of our entire ministry on the bridge was when we took the boys to a park area (Volunteer's Park,) next to the river and were playing games and chatting with them. After a while, we became aware that some of the boys had disappeared and sadly we easily located them sniffing glue in a concealed area nearby. They tried to deny it, but I had seen them doing it. Reuben even joined them after I warned him that he would be excluded from the meal later. The boys then came out from their location and there was an equal split in terms of who had (Simon, Luke, Joshua, Reuben) and hadn't taken solvents (Joel, Paul, Adam, Mark.)

The ones who had taken the drugs were mingling with the others, but we explained that, because they had done this, they weren't allowed to come to the evening meal. Luke became really upset whilst I was talking, and having taken a book out of his pocket, he slowly and deliberately began tearing pages out of it and throwing the pieces in the river. I saw that it was one of our books: "The Greatest Story Ever Told."

At this point, I told the "good" boys that it was time to leave, as I wanted to get them away from the obvious temptations, and I could feel that something was about to boil over as the atmosphere was tense. As we started to leave, the "bad" boys followed us and tried to stop us from leaving. They were blowing solvents in the faces of those who hadn't taken any, and were calling us names and using bad words. They were inhaling heavily from bags that they produced from hidden pockets in their clothes. They followed us up the street as we tried to get away.

What happened next reminds me of something from a movie. I told the boys that were drug-free to speed up, so we walked single file at a rapid pace. The boys on drugs rushed along beside us and around the other boys, enticing them to take the solvents and swearing and shouting. Reuben shouted for me to look as he threw the flip flops I had recently bought him onto the roof of a building. The others copied him and also threw things we had given them on rooftops. This was getting out of control, as the boys were getting high on the solvents. They blocked our way and deliberately bumped into us as we tried to make good our escape. The local people looked on and wondered what on earth was going on, but maybe due to fear, did nothing to help us.

We were heading for the usual evening meal location, but I knew we would struggle to reach it without serious problems. As we were practically running now, I ran into a man that I knew from a local church, which was en route, and he invited us to take shelter in his church. We did this, running up the steps and into the main church building where many people sat. The other boys chased us up the stairs and squared up to us in the hallway. They were blowing their drugs around and using foul language. The church security officers escorted them outside. I had to specify which boys were with me and which were not. It was really a terrible situation. Outside we could hear them shouting and cursing, and they were specifically shouting personal things about me. We stayed in the church for a while and eventually, when we thought it would be safe to leave, we left with some security who escorted us across the road to the evening meal.

I was really shaken by what had happened and, as soon as we were inside, the boys appeared at the metal gated doorway shouting obscenities at me. I couldn't look at them and stood with my back to the door. Then it was all too much, and I burst into tears as I stood there, wondering what on earth to do. The good boys ate in silence, as they also hated the division and were torn in their loyalties. The bad boys were quieter, but blew solvents through the door. When the other boys went over towards them, they waved their hands around and enticed the others, as if they could cast a spell on them saying, "Come and join us, it's fun out here. You know you want to." It was really evil, but the boys inside didn't see it like that. They just thought it was funny and were laughing with them. This was one of the only times where I really felt the presence of evil through these boys and the drugs they were inhaling, and I knew that it was the devil who had hold of their lives.

Paul, at one point, gave some food through the bars to one of them, but we asked him not to do it again. I saw that one of the boys, Simon, wasn't with the others and had left. Reuben was sulking at the back, accusing me of favouritism and saying that my character had changed. He was one of the boys I had a strong bond with, and I definitely didn't want to exclude him. He just couldn't see that it was his own actions that had caused the consequences. The youngest boy, Joshua, was clutching at the bars and really screaming foul language, as if he was possessed by something. It was really scary. Zee's father eventually got really angry and shouted at them all to leave. They quietened down but remained outside.

We decided to leave early because of the trouble, but I was worried about how we would get past the boys at the door, especially as they were all now really high on the solvents that they had continued to take whilst outside. As we left, having apologised to the family who were very gracious, we walked in single file again down the street. The boys followed us, but they kept punching me in the arm and calling me "ugly." This wasn't the worst thing I had been called, but the repeated punching in the arm became really annoying, as was the way they tried to intimidate us.

When we got nearer to the bridge, I saw Simon sitting with Matthew (the leader.) I spoke to Simon, but he didn't want to talk to me. I wasn't sure if he was ashamed of himself or still angry for being excluded. I told Matthew what had happened, but he already knew as Simon had told him. He got really angry with the boys and shouted at them. Matthew didn't like his boys upsetting us and, if we had real problems, he sorted them out. The younger boys were afraid of him. It was just a shame that he was still inhaling solvents so regularly. We returned to the ship a bit shell-shocked, but came back the next day to do it all again.

22: My Favourite Day

We had been praying and hoping that, before the Logos Hope left, the boys would be allowed to visit as one big group. Originally, we were working on a plan to show the Jesus movie in Tagalog down by the bridge, but this just became more and more complicated. In the end, the Book Fair Manager suggested that we bring the boys to the ship to show them the movie. I asked if they could also have dinner, and this was agreed. We told the boys a few weeks in advance to ensure they made themselves available, and they started to get excited. We made it really clear that any boys who had taken solvents would be excluded with no exceptions. I prayed a lot about this, as I really didn't want to exclude anybody from this event. We weren't sure how many boys would come, but I estimated fifteen to twenty based on the numbers we had been seeing on the street on most days. I was sure we would get some extras due to the occasion. We also decided that this would be our last ministry day at the bridge with the book table.

One unexpected problem was that, on hearing this announcement, Simon stated that he wouldn't be able to come. He was leaving on November 1st to go home to his family who were going to send him to live with his Uncle in a different province so he could return to school. He told us that it was already arranged and that his Dad was going to collect him on November 1st. I realised that if Simon wasn't going to be able to come to the ship, we would have to do something special for him instead, so I prepared a gift bag for him to take with him with some items from the ship and memorabilia etc. I told him I would give it to him on the morning he was leaving and that we could escort him to the bus station. But, in the run up to his leaving date, he became more and more upset that he couldn't come to the ship with the others. In the end, he decided that he would go home after the ship visit. This was not the type of decision we wanted to encourage, but we couldn't do anything about it.

On this special day, 9th November 2012, we spent the whole day with the boys in preparation for the evening. We started on the bridge with our table as usual as it was to be our final day of ministry. Simon joined in the spirit of the day by giving local people Gospels of John and telling them that Jesus loved them. We played pickup sticks and other games on the ground near to the table. This was a gift from someone in the UK and we used it a lot. To begin with, I was amazed at how something so simple provided hours of entertainment for the boys. Then I realised that they didn't have any material things of their own, so it was the novelty value. We had also promised them before that we would buy all of them "Halo halo" before we left. So, after playing some games and taking them for lunch at the venue as usual, we purchased approximately fifteen "Halo halo's" and they sat on the steps at Volunteers Park, next to the river eating them. Even Matthew the leader was there enjoying his "Halo halo." After this, we bought flip flops for all of the boys without shoes so that they would be allowed on the ship.

We then played more games, including tag, which made everyone a bit wild and caused the boys to jump on top of each other and on top of me. Some of the crew just chatted with the quieter boys for the whole afternoon. We brought a couple of Frisbees and a

Football from the ship and were playing with these but, as we were playing near the river, they frequently ended up in it and the boys had to keep retrieving them. I recall towards the end of our games, Luke (15) stripping completely naked with his hands covering his dignity and complaining loudly having been nominated to get the Frisbee. It was a funny sight as he waded naked and still protesting into the dirty water to get the item. However, almost immediately after it was returned another boy had thrown it back in again. Luke refused to go back in as he was already dressed, so eventually Reuben went in wearing his shorts and also complaining. We ended up losing one of the Frisbees which floated away down the river.

Some of the boys climbed a nearby tree. Others climbed out and along a wall to a crevice on a ledge, where they sat and looked out over the river. I ventured to follow them, which caused great interest amongst the boys who had never seen me do anything like that before. The only problem was Adam followed too closely behind. When I couldn't find a foothold anymore, and tried to move back, his foot was in my foothold and I thought I would fall in the river! Paul was watching this whole thing with a perplexed look on his face, as a lot of the time I would be quite serious with them. Now I was climbing a wall and shrieking loudly about falling in the river! After a few seconds, Paul smiled and grabbed Adam, who didn't have a clue what was going on or the problem he was causing, and pulled him back and out of my way in the nick of time. On safe arrival back to the river bank, I composed myself and started laughing.

At the appointed time, just eleven boys and some of us were collected by a mini bus belonging to the ship. There were meant to be two buses, but one wasn't available, so we all squashed into one and some of the crew had to walk back to the ship. The nice thing was that, although some of the boys we had invited didn't turn up at the meeting point, all of our regular boys were there, including the two Muslim's. The boys wouldn't sit still and were jumping around in the bus because they were so excited. We made them sit down as we went past the security point, otherwise they might not have been allowed into the ship area. Some of these boys had never been into this area, as they weren't even allowed to cross the bridge from Olongapo into Subic Bay.

In the van a few of the boys had their hands and T-shirts up over their noses and mouths. I asked what was wrong and Paul indicated that he felt ill due to the air conditioning, which he wasn't used to. Joel also was ill, with the start of a fever that continued for nearly a week, so he wasn't his usual self. On arrival at the ship, the boys wanted to run towards the gangway, but they were stopped and given a short talking to by us about the expected standards of behaviour. They listened, and then promptly disregarded everything we had said.

In the lobby, we wrote down all of their names and gave them badges. Fortunately, many crew members were on hand to assist as we had prepared well for the event and knew that we would need a lot of volunteers to keep control. We tried to split them into groups of three for the initial ship tour, with the inevitable result that they wanted to swap and change groups to be with different friends. Two boys, Paul and Joel, had disappeared and I found them waiting in the clinic to see the nurse, as they weren't feeling well and had been escorted there by a well-meaning crew member. I joined them as the nurse was saying, "I don't really know what we can do here…" So I asked them, "Are you well enough for a tour of the ship?" They said "Yes!" straight away and didn't seem to understand how or why they had ended up in the clinic, so I just took them straight back up to join the others. I commented to the nurse that they were street boys who were used to fighting off various ailments and that they would be okay in due course. She tended to agree.

The tour was amusing, as we tried to have two crew members with each group of three boys. However, the boys kept sighting each other from various points on the ship and then running to different decks to try and re-unite with their friends. I told my group that they weren't allowed to go to the top deck as it is against the ship rules, but then, out of the corner of my eye, I saw another of the groups of boys already up there and two boys hanging over the railings. I shouted for them to get down and then saw the crew member that was supervising them running across the deck to catch up. They had obviously escaped. This resulted in one of the boys from another group shimmying up a ladder to join them on the top deck, which is definitely forbidden. It was all pretty hectic, but also quite funny as we struggled to maintain control. We took them onto the bridge to try on the Captain's hat and have photos taken, and then some of them sat on the deck to watch the sunset. Next, they went to the Dining Room for juice. The ship juice is made from powder and is brightly coloured, so they all had coloured moustaches around their upper lips as they insisted on drinking more and more of this juice which really tastes bad. It was the novelty value I guess.

After the tour, a ship security person, who will remain nameless, approached me and told me that I needed to keep more control of the boys, and that we needed to stick to the "official tour route." I nearly laughed out loud at this, but just said that we would do our best. It was now time for dinner and the Chef had prepared rice and other items just for the boys, as rice wasn't on the menu for that day and most Filipino's eat rice morning, noon and night! The boys were allowed to go to the front of the dinner queues, but needed one crew member each, to assist them in getting their food, as they really didn't know what they were doing. All of the crew were really friendly and helpful. They had heard a lot about the boys and the boys were more than happy to talk to them. Once they had their food, the boys were directed to sit in a reserved area to eat.

At this point, I was made aware of a situation in the lobby area. One of the youngest boys, Joshua (10), had run away from his tour group and to the exit door leading to the gangway. He was now clinging to the door, crying, and refusing to let go. I tried to persuade him to come and eat, but he refused and became more and more hysterical. Eventually, I obtained translation and it turned out he was afraid that the ship would sail with them all still on-board and that they would then be our prisoners. He was really distraught. It took several people about twenty minutes to convince him that we would not sail with him still on-board and that we were not trying to capture him. Eventually, he came upstairs to eat and that was the end of that.

Whilst they were meant to be eating, the boys kept getting up and walking around the Dining Room, either to engage other crew members in conversation, or to take their chances and conceal various food items in their pockets for later. There was always a reason for them to get up and walk around, and of course heading to the "Comfort Room or CR" (a term for the bathroom in the Philippines) formed a regular part of their routine. One crew member went to the used clothes store on the ship, known as "Charlie," and collected some items of clothing to replace the ones that were really dirty or torn.

Eventually, it was time to watch the Jesus movie (in Tagalog) in a corner of the Dining Room. Most of the boys gathered near the front of the screen but some hung back, and Reuben wanted to sit on my lap. This was okay but as the movie started I felt a wet patch seeping through to my trousers, and after my initial surprise, as this was a 12 year old not a toddler, I gratefully remembered the earlier escapades in the river, so I asked someone to get him some dry shorts. The boys generally listened well and watched the whole movie avidly, although a few at the fringes of the group and Joel who still wasn't feeling well, fell asleep. In the middle of the movie, we overheard the following excited whisper coming from the two Muslim boys, Joshua and Luke, who were sitting at the front. Joshua said, "This is the part where Jesus is in the tomb for three days." He remembered this from an Evangecube that some crew members had been using on the bridge to share the Gospel!

After the movie, we let them take some sweets and soft drinks with them, and then we ushered them back down the gangway to the bus. Unbelievably, they were even more lively than on the way there! When we reached the city, we let them all out in an excited mass. They continued to hang on to bits of the bus as we were trying to drive away, and they were shouting and singing. I was glad I wasn't going to have to calm them down.

Although the bridge ministry, in terms of the daily presence of crew members with the book table seeking to share the Gospel, had officially ended, we still went to see the boys regularly and continued our feeding programme twice daily. Over the next few days, we began to see small punnets of jam, butter, and other breakfast spreads, in addition to Logos Hope wristbands, that had obviously been acquired from the ship whilst the boys were in the Dining Room and Book Fair. We accepted this as part of the course and were just grateful that they had been able to come after all the planning.

On reflection, although the event was stressful because I was co-ordinating everything, the rest of the crew really couldn't have made it easier for me. If I needed anyone to do something, everyone was more than willing, and it was obvious that all of the crew really cared about these street boys. I'm sure the boys could see that as well, and knew that this care was despite their bad behaviour. It was a real testimony that everyone on-board was patient and no one got angry with them.

23: New Beginnings

On continuing the feeding programme, we took the opportunity to invite the Christian couple, mentioned earlier, to come and see the boys, and also the Director of a local Christian Children's home. The idea was that, as the boys came off the solvents and started thinking about their lives and futures, they might be willing to study. And they would know that they needed to leave the street in order to do this. We had been preparing them for this during our ministry and always encouraged them to leave the street, go home, or go back to school. But we recognised that some of them couldn't go home for various reasons, so we wanted to provide an alternative option for them to consider. I was already arranging Sponsorship in the UK for them if they left the street.

I wanted Paul and Reuben to go to the Children's Home as I felt they would be able to deal with Paul's TB issues. I also saw that the two boys were close and almost like brothers at times. I thought that Joel and Adam might be suitable for the Christian couple, but I wasn't sure if they would be willing to consider two boys together as they already had six boys aged 16-21 and one girl aged 18 living with them. I repeatedly told Simon that he should return home to his own family, as he told us that he loved his family, although they were poor. Mark was also told to return home to his family, as we had done everything we could to assist him. I didn't know if we could help Luke and Joshua, the two Muslim boys, at this stage. There was only a limited amount we could do for the older boys, who really just needed to find jobs and stick at them, so we prayed with them to find work.

The Christian couple came and watched the boys playing. They spoke to Joel and Adam and agreed that they would return the following day, and that if the boys wanted to go home with them that they could. The family lived in New Cabalan which is up a very steep and long twisting road on the outskirts of Olongapo City. It requires two Jeepney rides, and about 45 minutes, to get to their house from the bridge area at a cost of 40 pesos (56p) return fare. They had been praying as a family about taking in more boys for some time and saw our ministry as God's direction and the right time for them to re-open their home. I was surprised that they would agree to this so quickly, but obviously excited at the prospect of two of our boys having a new home to go to. The Director of the Children's Home also came and witnessed the boys playing, and said that he would return at a later date for further discussion. He was willing to consider re-homing Paul and Reuben, although he was concerned that Paul had TB and the possible impact on their other children. I was thrilled as everything seemed to be coming together.

The following day, Adam went home with the Christian family, but Joel decided he wanted to stay on the street for now. We talked with him again, and he said that he would consider going the next day. Joel had developed a high fever after being ill for a few days. This was a part blessing in disguise, as he didn't take any drugs during this period because he felt too ill. We wanted to take him to the hospital, but he refused to go. The Christian couple came back the following day to collect Joel, but at this point Paul asked me loudly in front of them, "Ma'am Natalie, when am I going to go to the Children's Home?" I knew that he must be finding it difficult to stay on the street whilst not taking solvents, as it had been three weeks, and I was really proud of him. Immediately after making this statement he turned to the Christian couple and asked, "Will you take three?" They contemplated the request for just a few seconds before answering "Yes." Paul started jumping around and getting excited. They told him that they would come back again the following day to collect him. They took Joel home with them, which was a relief as I knew he would be looked after during his sickness.

Later, and privately, the family told me that they had taken the street boys out for a meal in a restaurant at Christmas time the previous year. They had photos of the occasion and I recognised several of our boys. They had at first been reluctant to take Paul, as they remembered his attitude and behaviour from the Christmas celebration. However, because he had asked them directly, they decided to give him a chance. I tried to reassure them that Paul was changing.

The next day, the couple appeared with Adam who had completely shaved his eyebrows off during a period of non-supervision, which caused a lot of mockery from the other boys! He was bouncing around and looked happy though, and it was a great transformation. One of the most noticeable things was that he was now wearing clothes that actually fit him instead of being three times too big. This was something the family enforced, with all of the boys, as a practical demonstration to them, that they were leaving their old street lives behind. It made a big difference to their appearance and made them look like young boys instead of gangsters.

They said that Adam had slept for most of the last few days. Paul took him outside for a quiet chat, and hounded him with questions about what it was like at the house. When he came back, he asked a series of questions of the Christian couple, based on the things he had learned from Adam. As we were leaving the evening meal venue, Paul took his TB medicine out of his pocket. This was quickly removed from him with the comment, "I'll take care of that. You have a Mum now." Paul repeated this to himself, "I have a Mum now."

I was walking with them and felt elated as we walked down the street to go and buy clothes for him. He was dancing as he walked past the loud music in the street. I knew I would be glad to see the back of the long baggy green T-shirt that I had bought him for 10 pesos (14p) before. He had asked me to buy him a T-shirt, as his was wet, so I agreed, but said it had to be cheap. He found a store where the T-shirts were only 10 pesos, so I offered to buy him a few as I was expecting it to be nearer 50 pesos (68p), but he said he only needed one. I noted the change in Paul, as previously he would have been likely to take the offer of extra clothes and then sell them, but now he was only asking for what he really needed and on this and other occasions he made sure that we weren't wasting our money on things they didn't need.

I was also looking forward to never again seeing Paul sleeping on the street, curled up in a doorway alone. Paul told us that, the previous year, he had been short but had just suddenly started sleeping thirteen hours a day and then grown really tall. For some reason, I always felt really sad when I saw him sleeping like that. Maybe it was because the other boys mostly slept in groups, but he was often alone. I guess seeing him curled up in a doorway reminded me that he had been cast aside like a pile of rubbish. He slept with his arms wrapped around his head, as if to block the world out. There was just something about this combination of factors that really made me sad, and I didn't want to see it again. After he left the street, I saw a boy curled up in a doorway exactly as Paul did before. I was filled with dread for a few seconds before I remembered it couldn't be him as he was with the couple now.

We went to the clothes store with the Christian family, but whilst we were inside, I saw Mark and Luke suddenly appear outside. They hadn't come to the meal that evening, and they were carrying solvents in plastic bags and were very high. Mark wouldn't speak to me at first and I knew he was angry with us. Then he said that we were trying to split their group up and that we were taking away all of their friends. He was really upset and was crying, as he said Paul was his best friend. Luke was more angry than upset, and also accused us of breaking up their friendship group by removing Paul. The two of them were really a sorry sight as they inhaled the solvents and stumbled around in the entrance to the shop.

Paul eventually came out with the family and looked at these former friends. I wondered what he would do, but I knew it wouldn't be a temptation for him as he had been clean for three weeks and he had a future to look forward to now. He walked to Luke and looked at him sympathetically. Then he just touched him on the arm and looked a bit embarrassed for his former friend, especially as they were behaving like this in front of the Christian family. Then he turned around and left them, walking off up the street after the family with a bounce in his step. I stayed with Mark and Luke and, as I watched Paul walk away, it was an emotional moment as he left his old life behind and headed for new things.

24: Division and Destruction

There were now three boys with the Christian family, and possibilities for some of the others. We arranged a collection on the ship to build an extension to the family home in order to accommodate the new boys, who had been sleeping in the kitchen. After a while, the extension was completed, adding an extra room and more outside living space to the house.

However, there were massive divisions in our remaining group of boys, and the real trouble makers were actively trying to tear everything down. The following day at lunchtime, Mark was really angry. He deliberately engaged us in an argument, accusing us of taking all of his friends away. He got really upset about this, and we spent time trying to explain to him that these other boys had no family to go back to. We reminded him that he had a family that he could return to at any time and that this is what he should do. It was hard to be patient with Mark at these times, as I kept remembering that he also claimed he was a born again Christian. Mark was causing us real problems and I was afraid of what he would do. He said that he missed his friends and wanted to go and see them. I told him not to go to the Christian family's house as he would not be welcome there. I also told him that his friends would come and see him when they were ready.

Mark worked himself up into a temper and stormed out of the building, telling Reuben to go with him. Reuben followed as, in their group, the younger boys have to obey the older ones, and Mark had placed his hand on Reuben's neck forcing him to obey. Reuben was uncomfortable with what Mark was doing, but he didn't really have a choice. Mark tried to flag down a Jeepney in the street, but they wouldn't take him as his clothes were so dirty. Reuben hung back and I tried to convince him to stay, but I believe Mark had already threatened him as he looked afraid. I told Mark again that he was not to go to the house, and then talked to him and Reuben for a while longer. In the end, I thought I had convinced them not to go. So we went back to the bridge.

Later, when we turned up to the evening meal, Joel and Adam were already there playing pool and Mark was sitting in a chair with a smug expression on his face. I walked straight over to him and told him to leave and that he was not welcome. I knew what had happened straight away and was really devastated at this turn of events, after all the work we had done convincing the two boys to live with the family in the first place. Mark had gone to the house and had taken Joel and Adam away with him. Later, Paul confirmed that this was what had happened and, on further questioning, also confirmed that Mark had offered them all solvents at the house. Paul declined and stayed at the house alone. Adam hadn't wanted to leave, but Joel persuaded him, as he was bored at the house.

I tried to speak to Joel and Adam, but Joel shouted that they had been told off at the house and that it was boring there. They didn't want to go back. They left together after Mark, who was still hanging around outside. I was so disappointed and upset with Mark. It was one thing for him to make choices about his own life, but he was 16 and he was dragging the younger boys down with him. The only thing that saved the situation was that Paul remained there and refused the very great temptation offered to him by a former close friend of his.

When the Director of the Children's Home came to visit our boys again, he was immediately concerned about Joel's fever. We explained that we wanted him to go to the hospital, but that he had refused. He asked if there was any other option, and we explained what had happened at the Christian family home. We added that we were trying to persuade him to go back to no avail. I told the Director about some of the problems we had been having with Mark, and he asked to have a private word with him. I was surprised but agreed, as by this point we needed any help we could get in dealing with Mark. I was also surprised when Mark agreed immediately to go with him and have a private chat, as I thought he would refuse. The Director later said that he would pray for Mark every day for a month. Mark's attitude changed after this and, although he had his ups and downs, he didn't try to influence the other boys in a negative way, which is the main thing we had been struggling with. I was really grateful to the Director for his intervention and wondered what on earth had been said!

We continued the feeding programme for a short time but found that the remaining boys were no longer serious about leaving the street for now, and we continued having to exclude some of them for drug use. I was also worried about the impact our ministry was having on Zee's family business as the boys would sometimes attend the premises "out of hours" asking if they could sleep in the doorway and with various other requests. The family dealt with the situation and the requests really well as they had started to love the boys as well. We learned that when trying to help these boys if we drew attention to a particular person or premises it was difficult to put reasonable boundaries in place because the boys were on the street 24/7 with nothing to do. The family didn't complain about any of the problems being caused and persevered with the boys throughout the ministry.

However, due to the problems, we brought the ministry to a close after a few weeks as we were also required elsewhere. After the conclusion of the ministry Zee's family really missed the boys and often asked how they were doing and sought them out to speak to in the street. During our ministry, they willingly and cheerfully sacrificed their time and home at virtually no notice, diligently collecting the food from the market daily and later preparing it. They even gave the boys vitamins for their health!

Such an example is sadly rare, but for us and the boys it was really a great blessing and the family will receive their reward later in eternity. I believe that although this feeding programme seemed not to have produced the desired outcome with all of the boys leaving the street, it was still the turning point in some of their lives. It was the first time they had been solvent free for more than a few hours and it gave them the chance to think about their lives and futures. Later we asked them why they had cut their drug use down so much and the vast majority of the responses were "because you were feeding us!" This proved definitively that the main reason for their solvent abuse was hunger. The response made the entire trauma worthwhile because we could see that we were slowly making a difference in the lives of these boys and that they were starting to make more sensible decisions.

25: Mixed Emotions

Eventually, we had to bring the bridge and feeding ministry to a close due to work requirements on-board the Logos Hope. Both of my Manager's had been very flexible and patient for a long time, but the time came when I had to get to grips with my job as Administrator of the Book Fair. Emotionally, I was totally exhausted and found that, although some tried, people on the ship really couldn't understand what we had been dealing with on the bridge. They told me to try and find a way to "let it all go" emotionally, as we would be leaving soon, but I wondered what exactly this phrase meant and how to do it. I had seen and been involved in things that had changed my heart forever. I had already decided that I wanted to return to the Philippines in the future, as I felt God's call in my heart and therefore I didn't see the purpose of letting go of what I had already experienced.

I hadn't even known where the country of the Philippines was before setting sail on the Logos Hope, so there was no hidden agenda on my part. I also had no idea that I would have a heart for troubled street teenagers because I had no prior experience of this type of work, apart from working for the police in England. Clearly, that was very different as we arrested the trouble makers and put them in a cell for the night. Now, here I was in a foreign country, at times, protecting the street teenagers from the police and other authorities. What a turn around.

Being removed from the ministry, however, did serve a purpose. It was good at that stage to have an emotional and physical break from the ongoing work with the boys, and to do something different. It helped me to gain some perspective and recognise that, even if just one of these boys really changed, it would be a miracle of God. I continued to pray for all of them but knew that my hopes and expectations for many transformed lives may be unrealistic.

Whenever the boys contacted me online whilst I was on the ship, I encouraged them to leave the street and go to the home of the family who had made it clear that they were willing to take any of the boys at any time. The Children's Home was still an available option, but they were only willing to accept children that were really willing to give everything and that really wanted to leave the street, not those who would keep changing their minds. I couldn't recommend any of my boys anymore, as they continued changing their minds daily.

During this time, I was encouraged that Paul remained at the house, although he was being difficult with the family at times and was extremely stubborn. The family brought him to the ship to visit us and it was really great to see him looking so clean and wearing nice clothes. He was even joking around with us and made the other crew members laugh as he didn't seem to know the correct use of many everyday items. At one point he did a demonstration of what would happen if he put his hand into an electric socket asking us if it was "10,000 volts "and then pretending to be electrocuted. I was pleased that he was smiling a lot and seemed relatively happy.

Soon after this first visit, Paul went to the street to find Reuben, and when he was located he encouraged him to join the family. Reuben agreed and went back to the house with him. This arrangement lasted for a while and the two boys came to see us on the ship with the family several times. However, both boys were increasingly stubborn, and Paul often contacted me on Facebook to complain about various things. Paul became jealous of Reuben because of the attention he was getting from the family, who seemed to like him more. The family admitted that they struggled with Paul because he was difficult and that they thought Reuben was funny, but I don't think they showed excess favouritism. Paul just needed that extra bit of attention and reassurance.

I went out for the evening with the family and the two boys and I could see that Paul was really unhappy. He refused to speak to me for the whole evening. The family managed to resolve things later, but I was upset by Paul's attitude as I was trying to help him. One of the things which I found really hard was that the boys constantly spoke about returning to the street and used this as a threat a lot of the time to get their own way. This was emotionally tough as I couldn't bear the thought of them being back on the street, but I couldn't allow them to walk all over us either. The threats to run away became reality several times as the boys jostled for first position in the household, but I told them to go back to the house and apologise, which they did at first.

Only a week after Paul and Reuben had joined the family, Simon also asked if he could join them and the family agreed. We had previously told Simon that he should go home to his own family, but as he obviously wasn't going to do this, it seemed better for him to go to this family than to be on the street. They took to Simon instantly since he was better behaved than the other two and polite. At this time, we decided to buy a special present for each of the boys at the house. We also obtained some books from the ship and other cheap gifts from Olongapo to try and give them extra things to do and to encourage them not to run away. We gave Paul a cheap cell phone with a camera, Reuben a skateboard, and Simon a bike. The gifts later caused problems as Mark forced Paul to give him his cell-phone and then sold it, Reuben didn't know how to use the skateboard and wanted a cell-phone instead, and the bike broke. However, for a while they enjoyed their gifts, and the initial excitement when they first received them was really great to see.

The three boys came to the ship several times with the family, but almost always got into some sort of trouble because they kept running around. I offered to take the boys around the ship for a tour, but when we began they were really naughty. They ran away from me and took things in the Dining Room. They wouldn't listen to anything I said and kept walking off. Paul ran away down a flight of stairs, only returning after about ten minutes. I was really angry due to the security lapse, which could potentially get me into trouble, so I really told him off. I dragged him and the other boys back through the door to where the family was waiting and told them what had happened.

The family told them off and said they needed to apologise to me, but this is really hard for a Filipino child (more so than in a Western country,) as it causes shame for them. They began to say one by one that they wanted to go back to the street rather than face me and apologise. I couldn't believe it, surely a simple apology wasn't too much to ask, but they would rather jeopardise their opportunity to stay with the family. I asked them how they thought the family felt every time they made these threats in an attempt to hurt me.

Eventually, all three boys apologised but it was hard work! I then took them on another tour, which was much more civilised, but I realised that they still hadn't made definite decisions to stay off the street so I lived in constant fear of them running away.

26: My Big Mistake

Joel asked me one day if I could take him to visit the other three boys at the house. The family obviously didn't want him living there again. (You will recall that Joel and Adam ran away from the family home within two days of their arrival after Mark took solvents to the house.) The family also said later that, whilst Adam was at the house, he had been caught smoking and rummaging through someone else's pockets in one of the bedrooms. It was Joel who had persuaded Adam to leave, but the family didn't want either of them back. Joel had been good for a few days, was pleading with me, and seemed just to want to see his friends. I decided it would be okay as deep down I felt sorry for him. This was a big mistake.

 When we got to the house, Joel said sorry to the family for running away and for his previous attitude. They forgave him straight away and said he could stay again if he wanted to and he agreed. They really were very gracious towards him in light of what he had done. But, despite Joel's apologies and promises, there was a lack of real sincerity and it was clear that things weren't right. Shortly after we arrived, there was an atmosphere of trouble. Joel encouraged Reuben to smoke, and Paul started a fight with Reuben after getting angry about something and hit him really hard.

This all calmed down and the boys went to play basketball nearby. However, when we went to call them for dinner, they began walking hurriedly away from us. When we speeded up to catch them, they started running with Joel at the helm. All of the boys followed Joel and started running off down the main road back towards Olongapo City. I was angry with Joel as we pursued them as I realised I shouldn't have trusted him or taken him to the house. We shouted for them to come back and followed for a while, heading along the Highway. Paul stopped running and turned and looked at us, seemingly caught in a dilemma, but he came to the right decision and began walking slowly back towards us. He came back to the house with us, but Reuben and Simon had left with Joel, I really couldn't believe it! We then broke the news to the family. They took it quite well, but I felt really bad as I knew Joel had deceived me. Later I asked Joel why they had run and he said it was because we were chasing them!

After a few days, the family were in a Jeepney in the city when they saw Reuben being chased by DSWD. They called his name and he ran and jumped into the Jeepney with them, as an alternative to being sent to Rehab. We also located Simon and Joel one morning asleep on some cardboard. As we approached them, Simon woke up but Joel remained asleep. We had been worried for some time about the influence of Joel on the other boys. It was clear that, even though they were a similar age, Joel was the leader of the younger group and they were afraid of him. We heard stories of him slapping them whilst they were asleep and stealing their money. We told Simon that this was his opportunity to leave Joel asleep and go back to the family. I didn't really think he would do this, but immediately he got up and said, "Let's go now." So we quietly ushered him away from the sleeping Joel. This particular incident was amusing, as it felt like we were stealing something or doing something we shouldn't, but really it was ridiculous. We shouldn't have been afraid of Joel , a 12 year old boy.

Having sneakily returned Simon to the house without Joel's knowledge, he ran away again only a day or so later and only agreed to go back if he could take another Muslim boy Joshua with him. The family agreed to take both of them, and so ended up with four of our street boys. I warned them that Joshua had stolen from me before, but it seemed to be a good solution for him to keep him off the street. We were told later, by some former neighbours of Joshua's family, that we should keep Joshua safe to protect him from his family who were cruel to him.

I asked a local church leader if he would look after Luke (the other Muslim boy) for us and visit his family when the ship left, as he was the only boy we really hadn't been able to help. I had been in discussions with the Director from the Children's home about Luke because they said they had had Muslim residents before and that this wouldn't necessarily be a barrier. But eventually Luke's family moved to Manila and we didn't see him again. I spoke to him a few times online when he first moved and he said that he still wasn't going to school and that he wanted to come back to Olongapo. I didn't hear from him again after that.

As the ship was preparing to leave Subic Bay, Joel and Adam were the only two boys left on the street from our original group, Joel contacted me online after a while and said that he really wanted to change his life so I went to speak to them in the city. When I found them, they were doing paid work and weren't really interested in talking to me, so I left. This often happened. The boys said one thing online and, when I tried to speak to them, they had forgotten because they were high on solvents at the time or had changed their minds.

Before the ship left I had a final conversation with Joel. He was sitting on the ground with a whole gang of younger boys. He was obviously miserable, as his friends of the same age were now living with the family, forcing him to hang around with younger children. However, persistently stubborn, he said that the group hadn't needed our help in the first place and that all we had done was destroy their friendships. He accused me of favouritism saying, "It's okay because I know you never really liked me or Adam in the first place." I told him that this wasn't true at all, that it was due to their behaviour that they had had problems and reminded him that they had had the same opportunities as the other boys. He spoke of another girl from the UK that had helped them once. He said that he knew that she was the only one who loved them and cared for them. It hurt me to see him like this, but I couldn't give him another chance with the family, because I couldn't risk jeopardising the other boys at the house, so I had to just leave him there on the street, which was really hard.

Overall, I was happy, as all of our boys had now had an opportunity to leave the street if they wanted, and this was one of our main goals. All four boys wanted to stay with the family and were adapting to family life as the ship was about to leave. However, the incidents of running away and returning continued and we found ourselves almost daily having to take one boy or another back to the family after various disputes.

The problem was that the bonds between the boys were so great. We were constantly fighting for control and to separate them from the only family they knew, their "street" family, because of the negative influence they had on each other. This was an emotional rollercoaster for me. The elation of getting one of the boys to leave the street, only to find a few days later that he had run away again, was very hard to cope with. I knew that the boys would only truly change if they made the decision to leave the street themselves rather than being put under pressure, but it was hard to watch them making bad choices and then suffering the consequences.

27: Final Farewells

The family visited the ship a few times with all four boys, even bringing them to a Sunday church service on-board. During the service, three of the boys promptly fell asleep, lounging all over the chairs. They only woke up for the singing, joining in loudly and out of tune. In the service, Paul drew something on a piece of paper and afterwards I read what he had written: "Jesus loves Paul", "I love you Lord", "Paul loves Jesus and Natalie", "God is my guide", and other similar things. I photocopied the page, as it was such an encouragement from one of our toughest street boys.

We visited the boys at the family house several times, including the day before we were due to leave with the ship. We had a great time messing around and laughing with the family. Whilst we were eating, I told Reuben that he needed to eat more because he was a growing boy. Simon helpfully translated this to him, but everyone burst out laughing. He had translated my comment as, "She thinks you are very wise because you have a big head." Then Paul told me off for leaving rice on my plate, as leaving food was against the house rules. I acknowledged this, as I wanted to be a good example to him, and told him it was the same at my house in England.

Later Paul was joking around and kept grabbing me and putting my hands behind my back in a police move that I had foolishly taught him before. Then he said "Police arrest" and refused to let me go as I struggled for freedom. Everyone else thought this was hilarious as I was screaming from being tickled. I was a bit worried. I knew I shouldn't have taught the boys these things in case they used them on other people and really hurt them.

As we were leaving the house for the last time, Paul asked me for one of my wrist bands with the Bible verse "With God all Things Are Possible." Matthew 19 vs 26. I gave him a blue one, but he gave it to me and asked for the black one I was wearing. Then he told me that when I came back to the Philippines we could swap back. I knew this was his way of reminding me that I had promised to come back. I said "Ingit ka" as I left which I thought meant "Take care", but he looked confused and started laughing and repeating it. It actually means, "You are jealous." I should've said, "Ingat ka!"

The following day, December 11th 2012, the family brought the boys to the shipyard to say goodbye to us, as it was to be our last day in port. All four boys were looking well but sad that we were leaving. The other crew members and some local people were really amazed at the transformation as they saw the boys playing on the quayside and recognised them from the street in Olongapo. Later Paul, unaware that he was being observed, played a game with a small boy on the Quayside. He covered up his eyes and pretended to be crazy, then went back to normal. The small boy was giggling and they were repeating this again and again. I thought back to when we had first met Paul: what a different boy he had turned into!

After that, I was sitting on the Quayside, with some crew members, on a stack of wood quite high off the ground when Paul approached me and grabbing my legs said "Ma'am

Natalie, I will miss you so much," unfortunately this caused me to lose my balance and fall forward off the pile landing with my bare feet very close to some metal spikes protruding upwards from the ground. I just crouched there for a few seconds feeling thankful for the exact final positioning of my feet!

Reuben was sulking and kept looking up at the ship, shaking his head, and looking really miserable. I knew it was because we were leaving and I felt sad for him. Later, the boys trailed home after the family as we said goodbye for the last time.

Once they had gone and I was back inside the ship, a Filipino crew member approached me to tell me about a conversation she had been having with one of the boys outside. The boy was talking enthusiastically about wanting to study and to get on with his life and other things. I knew she was talking about Paul, and hearing this made me cry, because of everything I had been through with him on the street and because I knew that, out of all the boys, he was really serious about wanting to change. I knew I would miss the boys when we left and I thought this was the end of the emotional goodbye. Not so.

A few hours later, whilst I was in the queue for dinner, I heard my name being paged to contact the gangway. Everyone in the queue looked at me surprised. Shore leave (permission to leave the ship to go on-shore) had already been withdrawn as the ship was about to leave, so it wasn't a good time for visitors! When I went to the gangway and looked out, there were Paul, Reuben and Joshua again. I just stood at the top of the gangway and put my head in my hands as I asked myself whether I could go through all of this again, but I couldn't just leave them there. I asked for permission to go down the gangway, which was granted. I went to hug the boys and say goodbye again. I couldn't understand why they were there, as I had seen them leaving with the family earlier, but now they were alone.

They said Simon had already run away from them, throwing his shoes in the air and shouting that he was returning to the street. One down and we hadn't even left yet! I made all three remaining boys look me in the eyes, promise to stay at the house, to be good, and to study hard. They all did so, but I knew it wouldn't hold them to anything. After a while, they left because it was getting late. In the end, the ship didn't leave until the following day. I was half expecting to look out of the window and see them on the Quayside again, or to be paged in the middle of the night to go to the gangway. I would gladly have stayed behind. The next few months were to be very difficult.

When the ship sailed away from Olongapo, I knew I had left part of my heart behind. It wasn't so much about the place, but about these boys whom I had come to know and love. I knew that some of them didn't have anyone who really cared for them and that, for a time, I had been that person. I hoped and prayed that they would remember that Jesus loved them more than me, and that they would look to Him now that I had gone.

Simon did go back to the house temporarily, after contacting me on Facebook and saying he was sad. The family arranged private tutoring for all four boys together, but they had just two lessons before things went wrong. It seems Joshua wanted to speak to the tutor about something, but she was busy with one of the other boys and he didn't want to wait, so he shouted for attention. When this didn't work he flew into a rage, screaming, shouting, and threatening to burn down the church where they were holding the lessons and to smash all of the windows. He then ran off, followed by Simon who said he was going to get him back.

After a few days on the street, Simon and Joshua returned to the family together. They were dirty, tired, and hungry, but a few days later they ran away again, each time with new clothes and shoes that the family had generously given them. Shortly after this last incident, Joshua's Muslim family moved to Manila. I haven't had any contact from Joshua since, although I have recently been told he is back in Olongapo City.

I remained in daily contact with the Christian family via email and Facebook. But I was constantly receiving messages from the boys to say they were running away or were sad, which was playing havoc with my emotions. The boys told me their complaints online but I couldn't do anything about it because we were now in a different country. In the end, I had to discipline myself not to check my Facebook account regularly because I couldn't deal with the ups and downs of the boys' lives.

By Christmas time 2012, just two weeks after the ship had left Olongapo, Paul was the only boy left at the house. The others had run away. The family was especially worried about Simon, as there had been an indication that he had some kind of health problem and he wasn't looking well when they had last seen him.

Reuben left because he didn't like the house rules and wanted to play outside at night. The family obviously didn't allow this, so then he stopped coming home. He ate regularly at a neighbour's house, but eventually, the neighbour said to him, "Why are you here? You're not part of this family." This upset him so he went back to the Christian family home, but subsequently got involved in a fight with a gang in the area and threw a rock at the head of one of the gang leaders. They threatened to kill him if he ever came back to their area. The family tried to smooth things over to no avail. He was like a wandering animal with nowhere to call home. When I heard this story, I immediately thought back to the gang fight, with the students, many months before, and was relieved that I had intervened, as this proved that Reuben would quite happily have thrown a rock at one of the students that day.

After New Year, Paul left the house twice after arguments, and on one occasion returned to the house having taken solvents and was told to leave again. However, in early February, he left after another argument and was caught the same day by the DSWD who by this point had obtained a Court Order for him to go to Rehab. It seems they were holding off enforcing the order whilst he was living with the family but his unwise decision to leave had consequences this time. He was quickly transferred on 6th Feb 2013 to Rehab in Manila. This effectively put a temporary end to everyone else's efforts to help him.

28: Rehab

A couple of months passed and many teams were preparing to head out from the ship during the April 2013 dry dock in Hong Kong. Many of the teams being sent out, were also going to the Philippines. I requested to be part of a team going to Olongapo, praying that if it was right I would get it. Although I had decided a few months before that I would return to the Philippines after I finished my commitment with the ship, I had started to doubt this during my absence from the country and needed confirmation of my calling. I was hoping this would be it. If I returned to the Philippines, I prayed that I would just know if it was right. The teams were assigned and I was allocated to a Philippines team, but to Manila instead of Olongapo. At first I was disappointed, but then I realised that I might be able to visit Paul and Adam in Rehab (Adam was transferred there after being picked up by DSWD in March.)

I was assigned to a team of six going to a poor area of Manila for the month. When I looked at the map, I saw that it was just one hour away from the Rehab facility. It was a big thing to ask my team leader and the host of the church we were staying in if I could take a day out to visit the boys. However, when I explained the situation, they were more than happy to let me go on one Saturday and even provided me with a translator from the church. So we set off, not really knowing exactly how to get there, but eventually arriving safely at the Rehab Centre in Manila.

The centre is primarily for adult rehabilitation, but they also house sixty to eighty children from age 11 to age 18. This Rehab is the only government institution in the entire area that houses these children. DSWD's from miles around obtain Court Orders to send their problem "rugby boys and girls" there. Olongapo is one of the most distant provinces to send children to this centre, which causes its own problems. The boys are transferred from their local province en masse and then spend a minimum of eight months being rehabilitated and going to school at the centre. Sometimes they are neglected or forgotten by their own DSWD, (out of sight out of mind), but that DSWD remains responsible for their welfare, including providing clothing and toiletries because the Centre itself doesn't have a budget for this. This is just one of the unworkable rules that I encountered.

The security at the centre is tight and very similar to a prison, with many guards, searches on entry, and lists of banned items including menthos and full length toothbrushes. Bizarrely, with the latter item, they snapped them in half, which seemed to create more of a weapon than before if that is what they were worried about. There is also a strict dress code. In fact, if you turn up wearing trousers that have a two inch gap at the bottom where your ankles are, you will be refused entry. The reason for the code is less clear, as the inmates wear shorts.

In the Philippines, many security and legal procedures seem to have been copied from the West, but as the purpose behind the procedures is sometimes not known or is interpreted incorrectly, these things become unnecessarily inflexible and bureaucratic. The officials almost always stick to their brief, even if it doesn't make sense or is not fit for purpose. There are few opportunities to complain and things are rarely addressed effectively or changed if you do. It is just part of life, but can be frustrating, especially when you are not trying to do anything illegal and are trying to help people.

On this, my first visit, after going through security and other bits and pieces, myself and my translator, were ushered to a large open area with tables and asked to wait for a while. Then, a social worker came and asked for the names of the boys that I wanted to see. I listed all of the boys that I knew, in case there were others somehow there, but I really was only expecting to see Paul and Adam.

After waiting for a while, I saw them coming towards me and, the biggest surprise of all, Joel was with them! I was saddened by their appearance; their heads had all been shaved and they looked thin and miserable. They huddled together in a small group as if they would find safety there and they were herded by some older boys. They looked dazed, confused, and very lost. Joel burst into tears when he saw me, and he and Adam both came over straight away and hugged me. Paul also struggled not to cry, as I tried to hold my own emotions in check, as I knew it was important for them that I remained in control. I was so surprised to see Joel, who had only arrived three days before my visit. All hostilities from before were completely forgotten now. I couldn't really speak much Tagalog, so I just asked them what they were doing and they said they were cleaning every day and were very unhappy.

We sat for a few hours chatting and ate some snacks we had brought for them. I also brought Bibles, many children's books, toiletries, clothing, and other items which they were very excited about. Interestingly, the thing that Paul and Joel were most concerned about was that their Facebook profiles might be deleted due to inactivity on their accounts. I was incredulous when they mentioned this, as that would have been the least of my priorities in a place like Rehab, but, again, it demonstrated their immaturity in setting priorities and reminded me that they were just children. I agreed to hack into their accounts using the passwords they supplied, just to keep their accounts active, but thought they would forget about this in time. On subsequent visits, the subject was mentioned several times. I was reluctant to hack into Paul's account because previously he had had a disgusting pornographic image as his cover photo. I refused to become friends with him until this had been removed. After initially claiming he didn't know how to change it, he had succumbed when my friendship became more important than his street credibility. Joel created a wanted poster of himself with the caption "Wanted: Dead or Alive" as his profile picture, which was less offensive.

The boys asked for some other things too and, as there was a small shop within the Rehab compound, I bought them everything they needed, which wasn't a huge amount in monetary terms. I was desperate to try and improve their lives a little, but I was irritated by the attitude of the guards manning the shop who kept trying to get me to buy more and more items. They suggested to the boys that they might need various items that they clearly didn't.

The boys told me that Adam had already been in trouble for fighting and that they had had no other visitors. They told me too that there were some boys and girls there who had no visitors for their entire year at the centre, which really made me sad. I determined to try and change this. We finished our visit after a few hours and said goodbye. I promised to visit again when I was able, but I wasn't sure when that would be as the ship schedule was still unclear and subject to change. I remained cheerful until we got outside, but then was in a daze for the rest of the day, appalled at what I had seen.

Thinking about the situation at the Rehab later, I thought how terrible it must be for children of that age to be in a prison type of environment, far away from everything they knew with no friends or family to visit them. The boys that did have families in Olongapo wouldn't get visits as their families wouldn't be able to afford to travel to see them. This was one of the main reasons for them being on the street in the first place: Poverty. It was a vicious circle. At first I felt completely helpless as I didn't see what I could do, so I spent the next few days crying every time I thought about the boys alone there without any friends or visitors. After a few days, I contacted the Christian family and asked them whether they would be willing to visit the boys once a month in the centre if I arranged funding for the visit from the UK. They agreed to this almost immediately and I was just so grateful. But this didn't help the other boys and girls who were there.

I wondered about mobilising local churches into some kind of visitation scheme to encourage long term relationships with some of the children without family members. But I knew this would be a lot to ask the local community, especially as I had no contacts or connections in the area. There was also the issue of confidentiality of the children to contend with, and the fact that some were from other faiths. It was just the beginning of an idea that might also help to solve the problem of these children leaving Rehab and going straight back to the street afterwards. This was really a big problem. The government spent a lot of money rehabilitating these children for a year and then some of them were ending up back in the Rehab for the following school year, having only just been released, because the underlying causes of their solvent abuse hadn't been addressed. They returned to problem families and abusive home situations in many cases. I thought that maybe it would make a difference if they had a more stable connection with a Christian on the outside.

I started by writing a letter to the DSWD Head Office for the area and also to the Governor of the Rehab. I requested permission to begin a visitation scheme by mobilising local churches. I explained in the letter how I would deal with the confidentiality and other faith issues, and how the scheme would benefit the children. I waited several months, but didn't receive an official response. Eventually, I received verbal permission from the Governor at the Rehab, but nothing from DSWD. It was difficult to do anything with this idea at this stage as I was back on the ship and we had moved to Hong Kong, so the idea was put on the back burner.

29: Bonus Visit

Originally, before the very long dry dock in Subic Bay in 2012, the Logos Hope was due to visit several other ports in the Philippines. Due to the extension, the ports were postponed to a later date. It was decided we would now visit these additional ports of San Fernando and Puerto Princesa. This was a great surprise for me as I thought these ports had been cancelled and, due to the amount of time we had already spent in the Philippines, I didn't think we would go back there so soon. The ship's community was divided over this decision with half of the crew wanting to go back as they had developed a heart for the country, and the other half never wanting to see the place again, even on a map due to the trauma of the conditions they had experienced during the long dry dock.. It was at this point that some people's true motives for being on-board were exposed as some complained that they were not experiencing enough different cultures or countries!

We arrived in San Fernando, Philippines on May 24th 2013, and I immediately made plans to visit Olongapo and the boys in the Rehab in Manila eight hours away! We only had a two week window of opportunity because Puerto Princesa, our next port, was on a separate island and required a flight to reach Manila or Olongapo. We had just seven days holiday a year on the ship, but I had saved most of mine, only taking a few days off when my parents visited, so I had plenty of capacity in this respect. I was disappointed not to be able to practice my Tagalog in San Fernando as the people spoke a different language, but as I was going on break back to Olongapo/Manila this didn't matter too much. My friends and former bridge personnel, Arlene and Nick, also wanted to see the boys so we travelled together on various buses and public transport for eight long hours to reach Manila. We stayed there for a few days and went to the Rehab on the Saturday, meeting the Christian family at the centre.

The boys were very excited to see all of us, as they hadn't been told in advance that we were coming. It was a great surprise, especially as I had told them I probably wouldn't be able to visit again until after I had left the ship. All three boys were still subdued, but seemed to have recovered from the initial shock of being in the Rehab. They all had scabies though, which hadn't been evident before. This was to be a recurring problem for them and for the centre, who couldn't afford to treat them properly at times. I made a big fuss about this in the medical centre because I hated to see the boys in this condition and constantly scratching. But there were no easy solutions.

Another issue for Paul is that, before he went to the Rehab, we had been working on getting his teeth fixed. His front teeth were all missing, having rotted away, which he said was from eating too much candy. We had paid for all of the rotten teeth to be extracted, and he was just about to have his new plate of teeth fitted when he got sent to Rehab. He was understandably complaining now that he was unable to eat properly, having had so many teeth removed. I went to the health centre within the Rehab compound with him and discussed this with a dentist. They didn't think it would be possible to sort this problem out at the Rehab although we offered various options to them, including paying for Paul to be taken outside with an escort from the Rehab to visit a local dentist. In the end, it was agreed that we would take a mould of his teeth and have the new ones created outside.

Actually, this never materialised, so Paul remained at the centre with no teeth for the duration of his time in Rehab. It reminded me of a time on the street when he said, "Ma'am Natalie, give me 100 million pesos." I replied, "What do you need the money for?" with no response from him. Then, he asked me for other amounts of money which I refused. On one occasion, he grinned at me with the big gap where his teeth should be very visible and said, "Ma'am Natalie....give me....teeth." which made me laugh.

It was also during this visit that Paul asked me to be his petitioner (legal guardian.) In practice, I was already sharing this role with the Christian family by attending to his health and medical needs. But I knew that I had to decline this request for several reasons. It wasn't clear whether he had biological relatives that would assume this role. There was a suggestion that he had a grandma somewhere who was still interested in caring for him. I was also not sure exactly when I would return to the Philippines and where in the Philippines I would be based. I was obviously not Filipino and only spoke very basic Tagalog. Being single, in addition to everything else, I felt that it would be the wrong thing to do.

However, I knew the underlying reason for the question. He wanted some kind of reassurance that I was not just going to disappear back to the UK, never to return, and that someone else in his life whom he had started to trust would therefore turn out to be a fake. I also knew that I must give him that reassurance, and that this was a serious matter for him. I told him that I would always be in his life in some capacity, and that I would ensure that he was cared for and looked after. I also told him that I loved him and all of the other boys and would do what I could to help them. This seemed to satisfy him.

The boys told us that all of the things we had given them on the previous visit, with the exception of the Bibles, had been stolen by the other boys at the centre, and that it had caused some fights. They quoted some Bible verses from memory, which was encouraging. The reason for the problems was that they hadn't yet been allocated any storage space to put anything in. The lack of even basic supplies in the sleeping area meant that all of the boys were desperate for things like soap and toothpaste. Again, I purchased the things they asked for in the canteen area, including basic footwear and shorts/T-shirts. These are required to be worn as a uniform, but the centre doesn't have a budget for them, so the boys have to purchase them themselves! They all wore borrowed clothes, which they said they had to return, and some of their clothing had holes in it. One of the boys had a twisted wire in the bottom of his shoe to hold it together. All of the boys were complaining that they couldn't sleep properly because they were all in one big room on the floor with no bedding. They said that the room was dirty, resulting in the scabies.

We gave all of the supplies to the social worker this time to prevent thieving. Then she asked me whether, instead of just helping our boys, we could find a way to help all of the children at the centre. I felt a bit helpless at this request and explained that, as we were missionaries from the ship, we didn't really have funding for that type of thing, but I said that I would do what I could. She just smiled at me patiently and I left feeling convicted.

Afterwards, I really felt angry that a government centre would house children in these conditions without basic cleaning products, and without proper access to medical/health facilities. Over time, I was often asked for "donations" to buy basic products for the centre like cleaner for the rooms etc. I had to weigh each of these requests individually and make decisions based on how necessary the items were for the wellbeing of the children. To begin with, I said "I'm not going to purchase these items because it's the government's responsibility and it will just encourage them not to budget for the things next year."

However, after a while when these things were not purchased if I didn't donate them I wondered whether there really was an issue with money. Of course, the real problem is the corruption at the top of the chain but, ultimately, by refusing to help the government staff at the centre, I was actually refusing to help the children who were the ones to suffer. So, over time, I became more willing to help, even if it was someone else's responsibility.

30: Good News and Bad News

After the Rehab visit, we went to Olongapo for a brief stay of only two days. Due to the short duration, the three of us rushed around to meet various people and to try and find the remaining boys still on the street. We located Simon one day, and I was shocked by his altered state. I had been warned by the family that he wasn't well and they had been trying to get him to go to the hospital. He had lost a lot of weight and was limping badly. His eyes were dull and dead and he just looked ill. He came rushing to us and gave me a hug, but I just couldn't believe his appearance. I was really upset, especially when he couldn't catch his breath when he was talking to me and I could hear some kind of wheezing. I told him that he needed to come to the hospital with us, but he didn't want to. Reuben was similarly dirty, but seemed livelier. He didn't want to speak to me and just stayed away from us. I had been close to him so this upset me, but there wasn't time to really find out what the problem was.

Later as we were walking with Simon and Reuben, we met Mark's mum working and she seemed really happy. She told us that Mark had finally re-enrolled at school for his final year of high school, and that he had also enrolled his sister. He was going to school, living back at home, and there were no longer any problems. I was really amazed, but thankful that at least one of the boys had changed.

Later Mark was summoned and came to see us, and he really was different. He was very quiet and shy. He seemed almost embarrassed by our presence, but it was clear he wanted to see us. I asked him about the solvents and he said, "I don't want to do that anymore." Although I was really pleased for him, I couldn't help thinking about the younger boys that he had led back to the street. We knew that he wasn't really addicted to the solvents, as he was only taking them for a short duration and that he could stop at any time. My concern was for the others that he had led astray. Of course I didn't mention this to him. I knew that he had been desperately unhappy when making these mistakes and I believe that everyone deserves another chance if they sincerely decide to sort things out. I encouraged him to continue what he was doing, as he said he was also going to church and Bible study.

Matthew had moved in with Mark's family and was also living at their house. Although this was to be of short duration, it was good news because Matthew really didn't have a suitable family of his own. Matthew was working, helping Mark's mum, and Mark's dad was also coming home soon from his work abroad. I was encouraged to hear all of this news.

Before we left late in the evening, we managed to persuade Simon to attend the hospital with the Christian family. However, when they returned, their expressions were sombre. There was something wrong with Simon's heart and he needed to have further tests. They had arranged an appointment at the clinic near the bus station for the following morning, just before we had to leave to travel back to the ship. I didn't think there was any way that Simon would come to the appointment.

The next day we hurried to the bus station and, sure enough, Simon and Reuben were sleeping on the chairs outside the clinic. I was amazed to see this and it seems Reuben had been instrumental in making sure Simon kept to his appointment because he was worried about him. We left Simon having his tests with the family and travelled eight hours back to the ship. Later it was confirmed that Simon had an enlarged heart, probably due to his abuse of solvents, and that he needed to take daily medication, perhaps for the rest of his life. If he didn't take his medication and continued inhaling solvents it would likely be fatal for him. This news was really devastating. To begin with, Simon agreed to go home with the family to try and get better and have his treatment. Reuben encouraged him to go with them, but refused to go himself.

31: Logos Hope Returns

When we got back to the ship there was a rumour circulating that there was a problem with the engine again and that maybe we wouldn't be able to travel yet to our intended destination of Puerto Princesa. The Director indicated that we might have to travel to another unnamed port in the Philippines that was closer to hand. People began whispering as the Director tried not to smile as he knew the impact this announcement would have. Subic Bay and Manila were mentioned by various people as everyone wildly speculated about where it would be. I thought that the Director wouldn't allow us to return to Subic Bay due to the psychological impact this might have on some of the crew members who had suffered greatly during the dry dock. In fact, most people didn't want to go back there and there were just a few of us that did. I just prayed that God's will would be done. When it was finally confirmed after a few days that we were heading for Subic Bay I was astonished, and I kept thinking it would be changed again. Crew members congratulated me as if I had had some personal success, but I couldn't stop smiling.

On June 11th 2013, I woke up late and looked out of the window expecting to see unfamiliar surroundings, as the leadership had told us we would be in a different berth to the previous one. But we were in exactly the same berth as before. It was totally surreal. I immediately arranged to visit the Christian family and was one of the first people down the gangway. I saw another crew member running outside and kissing the ground. This was a bit over the top for me, but I knew how he felt. It was like coming home. The only annoying thing was that we had travelled for eight hours each way to get to Olongapo and Manila just a week before. But this didn't really seem to matter now. It was unclear how long we would be staying for, but it wasn't going to be just a few days stop over.

Over the next few days I spent a lot of time walking around Olongapo City trying to find various boys. The former large group of "rugby boys" under the bridge were noticeable by their absence and this was commented on by many ship crew members. The city was almost eerily quiet for me as I walked the streets now. On prior occasions I wasn't able to walk more than a few feet without hearing "Ma'am Natalie" in an excited voice from one direction or another, before any number of boys descended on me. The lack of attention was bittersweet because I knew that some boys had left the street to go back home or back to school or were working, but I also knew that a few were still out there and had been driven underground by our activity and that still others were now in Rehab as a last resort.

One unintended, but mostly positive, side effect of our work with the boys was that during and after our ministry, the DSWD and police seemed to step up their activity and efforts to get the boys off the street. I cannot definitively say whether this was due to the heightened visibility of the boys because of our interest in them or just a coincidence in timing. Once the large group had been reduced to twos and threes the peer pressure problem became much smaller and easier for the authorities to manage effectively. This in turn made it harder for us to locate the boys as they no longer had the safety of the large group and were often hiding from the authorities. It wasn't as much fun for the boys to hang around all day with one or two others, and they quickly ran out of ideas to keep themselves occupied. They also started to have nagging doubts about their lifestyle choices, knowing that some former street friends were now back to their families and in school. They began to wonder if they would be "left behind." I preyed on these insecurities, for their own benefit of course, advising them that they would be "left behind" and alone as their friends headed for better things. I encouraged them to take the opportunities being offered to them as they wouldn't be available forever.

On one such occasion I tried to persuade Timothy a 14 year old former "rugby boy" that I knew, to leave his very low paid job selling toys at the market, for a place in a Christian Children's home and the chance of an education. This had already been arranged for him as the home were caring for his younger brother. As I was speaking, an older man happened to pass by and caught the gist of the conversation. To my surprise, as Filipino's tend to be shy especially in the presence of foreigners, the man intervened and began advising Timothy in strong terms that he should "grab the opportunity being offered with both hands." Sadly, Timothy refused at that time, but later he was taken in by a local social worker and is now doing well.

On June 15th we headed to the Rehab in Manila again for the monthly visit. On this occasion, we took Mark and Matthew with us. Both boys had remained off solvents, with Mark in school and Matthew working. We knew it would be a nice surprise for the Rehab boys to see them. We also took Simon with us for a visit because he wanted to see his friends and we wanted him to see what the conditions at the Rehab were like in the hope that he would make a definite decision not to end up there. The visit went well, with all of the Rehab boys talking to Mark and Matthew. Peter, also from Olongapo, burst into tears when he saw Matthew, so Matthew had to spend a lot of time consoling him. Peter had been at the centre for a long time with no visitors. We welcomed all of the boys from Olongapo into our group every month. The staff and other boys referred to us as the "Olongapo group" and arranged a large table for us to provide food and to spend time chatting with them. I wished there was a group like this for every City/area as it was something for the boys to look forward to every month and our large group became like a family gathering.

We celebrated Joel's birthday this time, having bought him a big cake. I didn't tell the others that, on the bridge, Joel had once told me that his birthday was in October and demanded that I give him a present. When I had refused, he got really upset and angry, so I gave him some jumping balls that I had in my bag as a gift and said, "Happy Birthday." He had accepted this quietly, but now I knew the truth and understood his response, as it hadn't been his birthday at all. But this time it was different, and I saw that Joel was changing. He said that he wanted to go and live with the family after Rehab, and they agreed.

We gave the boys proper sleeping mats that we had purchased. I wanted to buy mats for all of the children there using funds from the UK, but I needed some time to work out the details. I asked the social workers about this and told the family that I would get the money together if they could find something suitable. This was arranged and, during the visit in August, the sleeping mats were given for all of the children at the centre. This was to try and prevent scabies, and allow them to have a decent rest. They got up at 5am to start exercises and always looked exhausted whenever we visited them.

Again, it was hard to leave, but the boys were so used to seeing me turning up unexpectedly that they didn't believe it when I said I definitely wouldn't be back until the following year. When leaving, we told Simon he had to stay there, as a joke, and he looked horrified. We asked him whether he wanted to end up there as a resident and he said no and that it was a horrible place. However, in the van on the way back, he became restless and said he was going to run away back to the street again. I couldn't believe it, after what he had just seen. I really couldn't understand what was going on with this boy and thought maybe it was related to an actual addiction to the solvents, as it seemed the only explanation. I worried about him as I knew that he was undecided. A short while after the family got back, he ran back to the street again.

Back in Olongapo, I determined to locate Simon, who wasn't taking his medicine, and Reuben who had also run away from the family. I found Simon with another boy high on solvents, they were playing pogs in the street. They had a small boy, about three years old, with them and they were supervising the child, who was the brother of Simon's friend. I scolded them that they were in no fit state to be looking after the younger child. Simon told me he would go back to the family "tomorrow." The boys said this frequently, but we learned to interpret it as their intention never to go home. We learned that, if we wanted to make progress, we had to get them to do things then and there, otherwise it wouldn't happen. In the end, I had to leave Simon on the street, but I was so upset by his state of health that I couldn't sleep.

Another day, I found Reuben very dirty and sad, so I took him and his friends for food at a local restaurant as a peace offering. When I first saw him, he walked the other way and refused to talk to me. I went after him and said sorry for whatever I had done, and I told him I would buy him food. At first he refused, because he is stubborn, but when I started walking away with his friends, he joined us. One of the other boys, Samuel, I knew already. Samuel told me that Reuben was living at his house, which seemed like a good idea rather than him being on the street. I went to visit Samuel's family with the two boys to check out the situation and found that the boys were sleeping in a really small room at the top of a ladder. There wasn't much ventilation so it was hot, but at least Reuben was off the street, so I told him this was okay. I sat and talked with Samuel's family for a while. There were many children there and neither of the parents had work. Later, I arranged to replace a faulty light bulb so the boys could see upstairs, and I told the family that I would bring them a Bible.

I returned on another day with the promised Bible and saw Reuben knocking a tree with a wooden stick to try and get the fruit on it to fall on the ground. He was very subdued. I gave Samuel's family the Bible and prayed with them. But they told me that Samuel refused to attend school and they were worried about Reuben's influence on him. I supported Reuben staying there, as I didn't want to see him back on the street, but I knew that he had moved around from one house to another over the years and always ended up back on the street, which he described as his "home." When I left, the boys convinced me to buy them flip flops because Samuel's were broken. Reuben promised that he wouldn't sell then but later broke his promise and then left the house for the street once again.

On our last day in Olongapo, I saw Reuben high on solvents, alone, and miserable outside a pub. He refused to speak to me still, and I was sad. I spent twenty minutes trying to persuade him to leave the street, and telling him that he would end up in Rehab otherwise, but he just ignored me. I told him then that I would report him and the other boys left on the street to DSWD. I had no choice, as I couldn't stand to watch them destroy their lives anymore. I hated to do it, as I knew it could damage the relationships I had built up with the boys if I reported their locations to their "enemy", but I felt I had no alternative. I asked the family to inform DSWD about the boys before I left Olongapo.

32: Miles Apart

When the boys were taken from the street by DSWD, the first place they were taken to is the Centre for Youth in Olongapo. This was a government facility used to hold the boys, pending their transfer to Rehab or back to their families. It wasn't really suitable for long term housing, due to the lack of available resources. However, in the last year, the centre was completely refurbished by a foreign charity, making it possible for up to twenty boys to live there. There are staff on duty 24/7 and social workers are present during the day. The centre has changed a lot, and the charity also provides funding for days out and some other activities. Although there is still room for improvement, as the boys don't yet have a full programme, it is a good start. They will be starting to send the boys to school in June of 2014. The general rule is that the younger boys and those who behave well and don't run away can remain at the centre, but those who are known to be addicted to solvents and who try to escape will have their papers processed for Rehab in Manila.

Soon after the ship left Subic Bay for the last time, Simon and Reuben were caught by DSWD and taken to the Centre for Youth. The family visited them there, and the photos of them showed that all of the life had gone from their faces and they really looked hopeless. Reuben kept begging the family to take him home, but they had already decided that he needed to stay there as he kept running away, even though, at one point, he had been officially registered as their foster son. Simon was receiving his medical treatment, which I was asked to pay for a few times after hospital visits.

In the end, both boys ran away and, by the time they were recaptured, a Court Order had been processed for Simon to go to Rehab. It was agreed on the basis that I would fund his medical care whilst he was there. As I didn't see an alternative because we had tried everything else, I agreed. I couldn't believe Simon had been so foolish. He had seen the Rehab and what it was like, but still had thrown away a year of his life. Reuben was kept at the centre for some time, as he was afraid of going to Rehab, and he seemed to be settling down there. But eventually he ran away several times and DSWD obtained a Court Order for him to go to Rehab too.

The family continued to visit the boys for the next few months as I finished my commitment on Logos Hope, and I received regular updates and reports about what was going on. The group of people heading to Rehab for the monthly visit was getting larger as family members of the boys asked to accompany the family. Simon had an emotional reunion with his father and sister during one of these visits. Other boys were taken to Rehab using our "taxi service," and the family took some boys from the Rehab back to Olongapo on their release. I felt it was beneficial because the family were giving spiritual input to the boys and their families and maintaining the relationships with the boys during their captivity.

I received the following message, from the boys in Rehab, initiated by Paul, on September 5th 2013 which was my birthday. It has been translated into English:

"Dear Natalie, How are you? I hope you are fine wherever you are. Always take care and bear in mind that we love you. Thank you for taking care of us when we were still outside and it is because of you that we are out of drugs, also the family. Because of you, we came to get close to GOD. I hope, after our time here in the place of recovery, we could be together. I promise I will never go away again and I will never sleep in church. I will always listen to your advice."

This confirmed what the family had said, that Paul was taking his faith seriously in the Rehab. Later I was also given a beautiful swan made from coloured paper with my name forming part of the design, which had been made by Paul and the other boys. The staff members at the Rehab were trying to find ways for the boys to earn a bit of money, so they taught them origami. The gifts were really very good, but unfortunately the advertising and maybe the market weren't, so the project didn't really take off.

33: Olongapo Christian Help and Hope

The decision to return to the Philippines after my commitment on board Logos Hope had already been made. The question remained, where in the Philippines? I had been to Cebu, Manila, San Fernando, Puerto Princesa, and, of course, Olongapo. I had received offers of work from most of these places, but mostly in orphanages. People hear, "she works with street children" and they immediately think "orphanage" not "evangelist." This has been one of the stereotypes that I have had to fight since returning to the Philippines.

Essentially it boils down to this; Yes, I formed strong bonds with the street teenagers on the bridge. And yes, over time, I came to love and care for them not just as street children but as if they were my own children and I would've done anything to see them leave the street and the drugs. But, the ultimate goal has always been to see their lives totally changed by the transformation that can only come through Jesus, and the hope that is found in Him, not to make the children dependent on me or anyone else. God loves these children much more than I could and He understands exactly what is going on in their lives and why they make the decisions they do. He is the only one who can truly help them. At times, the poverty and need have been so overwhelming, and the situations so desperate, that practical help has become the priority for that time. But it remains true that a person can be given all of the food and material help in the world, but if they die without Jesus, they will spend an eternity in hell. After my time on the ship, my slogan became "Help and Hope must go Hand in Hand."

Leaving the Logos Hope after two years was a struggle for most people. However, I can honestly say that it wasn't for me. I had found the last few months on-board very hard as I waited to finish my commitment so that I could return to the Philippines independently. As our van left the ship, to head for the airport in the middle of the night in September 2013, I boldly shouted "Freedom!" causing everyone to laugh. Unfortunately, ten minutes later, we had to return to the ship after being pulled over by the police for making a wrong turn, and then realising that someone had left their laptop behind. Needless to say, the others blamed me for my premature jubilation!

Having said this, I learnt a lot of things on the ship, and am grateful to God for my experiences and the many ministry opportunities, and especially for the clear future path that was mapped out for me during my time on-board. This had been a major prayer request on heading to the ship in 2011.

Due to my relatively short time in the UK I don't think re-entry really hit me as it did some other crew members who had difficulties for months afterwards. Knowing that I would be returning to the Philippines long-term, and with "Help and Hope" in mind, during my few months in England, I set up a small charity called: "Olongapo Christian Help and Hope." The three official purposes of the charity are:

1. To advance the Christian religion in Olongapo, Philippines and the surrounding areas for the benefit of the public, through distributing literature and verbally sharing to enlighten others about the Christian religion.

2. The prevention or relief of poverty in Olongapo, Philippines and the surrounding areas by providing: sponsorship, grants, items, and services to individuals and families in need.

3. The relief of financial hardship among people living or working in Olongapo, Philippines and the surrounding areas by providing such persons with goods/services which they could not otherwise afford through lack of means.

In layman terms, the purpose is: to "Spread the Gospel of Jesus" and "Help the poor." This formalised the financial giving that had started in late 2012 when the boys went to live with the family. The bulk of the funds were now to be used for the monthly visit to the Rehab.

Once the charity was established, I put my affairs in order and sold nearly everything that I owned on Ebay, which was a challenge as I had been living in a three bedroom house. I ended up with just four boxes of personal effects! Then I prepared for a longer term return to the Philippines. After a few weeks in England I was desperate to get back to the ministry with the boys and away from the cold weather! I finally booked my flight and after fifteen and a half hours arrived in Manila on 12th December 2013 less than two months after I had landed back in England from the ship!

34: Centre for Youth

One of the first things I did when I arrived back in the Philippines was to visit the Centre for Youth to get to know the DSWD staff there. I had heard a lot about the centre from the Christian family and I wanted to see if any of my boys were there. When I first arrived, the social worker was quite cool with me. After I had been talking about the purpose of my visit for a while she suddenly said, "What did you say your name was?" and I said "Natalie." She smiled and said, "Oh so you're Miss Natalie!" She told me that a lot of the boys had been talking about me before, but most of them had now run away or were in Rehab. I was pleased that the boys had been talking about me in a positive way after some of the negative things that they had said to me in recent months. It proved that they didn't really mean the harsh things they said in the heat of the moment, and that they would always be happy to see me if I found a way to visit them wherever they were.

After this, the social workers were very friendly and helpful and shared information if it would help the boys. As mentioned in earlier chapters, my attitude towards DSWD in the past had been largely shaped by stories from the boys, as this was my only source of information. However, the Christian family had a good relationship with DSWD and, after leaving the ship, I started to see things differently as I heard about some of the good things that were being done.

On meeting the social workers personally, I was amazed at their levels of knowledge about the individual boys that I had been working with, as they had many years of experience in dealing with the families of these boys. It was useful for all of us to talk as we were able to fill in the gaps for each other. For example, they told me that in 2012 they had obtained Court Orders for Solomon and Luke to go to Rehab, but that they hadn't been able to locate the boys and so had been forced to cancel the orders. I told them that, during our ministry, Solomon had gone home and back to school and that Luke's family had moved to Manila. In turn, they were able to give me information about the family backgrounds of the boys which really helped me to understand the boys' behaviour better and to discern whether I should be persuading them to go back home or to the youth centre or to Rehab!

My first official invitation to see the boys at the Centre for Youth was to attend their Christmas party. At this time, I only recognised one boy, Malachi (9 years.) Unfortunately, Malachi kept running away from the centre and there is now a Court Order for him for Rehab too, despite his young age. On another occasion, Isaac had been captured. He looked miserable and was pretty non-communicative. He was one of the harder boys from the street, but he did acknowledge me. He asked me to bring some biscuits next time I visited. I was surprised when I received requests like this. Such small things seemed to have taken on such great importance in the lives of these boys. I was told that Isaac would be going to Rehab soon, as there were already court papers. A week later, another familiar face (Solomon) was there. He came up to me saying, "Ma'am Natalie, it's me, Solomon." I acknowledged him, and then he sat down in a heap looking miserable. I was especially sad to see Solomon, as he had previously left the street and returned to school. Both of these boys were due to be transferred to Rehab and wouldn't settle down at the Centre for Youth. Solomon even tried to saw the bars off the window during the night to allow an escape attempt.

At the centre, I had the opportunity to join a Christian programme with a local church, and we taught the boys the story of the lost son and the lost sheep. For the lost son, we played a game with balloons where bits of the story were inside the balloons and the boys burst them to make the story. For the lost sheep, I cut out an individual paper sheep for each of them, which they wrote their names and ages on. We played a game where they moved around the room to music and, when the music stopped, we called out a name from the sheep and they had to hug that boy. This descended into chaos quickly as they shoved and squashed each other, so we abandoned the game. Later, I hid the sheep outside for them to find their own. Isaac got very excited on finding the sheep with his name on it. He found it stuck underneath a table and shouted excitedly, "Hey look! I've found my sheep!" This response illustrated the parable well.

Another time, I shared the "Wordless Book" with the boys. This is a book of different coloured papers. The first is yellow representing heaven, then black for sin, red for Jesus blood, white for clean/new life, and green for growth. It is a really simple way to share the Gospel that I learnt on-board Logos Hope, and have used many times since. I avoided my usual error of asking the boys what makes them grow, and receiving the obvious answer of "food", by being more specific: "What makes you grow closer to God?" Afterward, I offered to paint the colours of the wordless book on their arms to help them remember the story. I had done this before and was surprised by how many of them wanted it, including the older boys.

My charity also donated many Christian books, Children and Adult Bibles in the local language to the Centre for Youth and some other local institutions. I told the staff that if the boys were leaving and wanted a Bible then they should take one and I would happily replace it. It is really important for them to have access to good quality Christian literature in their own language, especially as many of the boys don't speak any English and their entire library was in English.

35: Reunited

On 14th December 2013, I joined the family for their pre-Christmas Rehab visit. This was an event to remember as we hired two vans, due to the numbers of family members and other people now visiting, and prepared food and gifts as a special celebration. It was also a surprise for the boys as I had previously told them I wouldn't visit again until the following year and they had no idea I had returned early to Olongapo.

At this time, I met Joel's father, step-mother and one of his step-sisters, Simon's dad and sister, Paul's Grandma and some other relatives that accompanied us in the vans from Olongapo. It was a really great day. One thing that stands out in my memory is Joel's emotional reunion with his father, and him spending time playing with his step-sister. We had had to persuade Joel to allow us to bring his father as they were estranged. He agreed, on the basis that, if he told us where his family were living, we wouldn't make him go back and live with them again in the future. This was agreed, as a temporary solution, in the hope that Joel and his father would rebuild their relationship and Joel would change his mind.

A couple of things overshadowed the pre-Christmas celebration. Adam burst into tears when he saw that there was no one to visit him and cried for a long time. This surprised me because I hadn't realised how his lack of visitors was affecting him, as he had never mentioned it and he rarely showed this level of emotion. All of our attempts to console him failed, and I determined that we must bring him a visitor on the next occasion.

Paul sat with his "Grandma," but there was little warmth between them and they weren't really communicating properly. Later the social workers had family discussions with all of the relatives and the boys individually. I was informed that Paul's "Grandma" wasn't actually his Grandma; she was only a neighbour of his mother. As she was not related to Paul and was already old, she didn't want the responsibility of looking after him on his release and didn't want to continue visiting. Apparently, Paul's mother had given him to her as a baby and said, "Here, this is your son now." and just left him there. After this discussion, the lady didn't visit Paul with us again so we were unable to establish whether her story was true or whether she was just seeking to transfer responsibility maybe due to a lack of funding, a lack of interest or some other unknown reason.

 Discussions were already ongoing about where the boys would live when they left the Rehab. Joel and Paul wanted to go and live with the Christian family, Adam wasn't really sure, and Simon was going home to live with his father and sister in Olongapo. There was always the option for any of the boys to return and live at the Centre for Youth but where there were suitable family members that was obviously preferable.

During this visit, the social worker informed us that they had applied to the court to release Simon straight away, as they were unable to deal with his heart condition in the Rehab. My charity was paying about 1800 pesos (£25) a month to allow them to take him to the hospital for regular check-ups and for his daily medication. I was concerned that he wasn't being impacted by his stay in Rehab, as he didn't have to participate in the exercise programs and other activities due to his health problems. The other boys said that he was having an "easy ride." However, I was even more concerned at the prospect of his early release after just a few months as I could tell that he wasn't yet rehabilitated and despite his health concerns he would be likely to go straight back to the solvents and the street. I hoped and prayed that the release order would be delayed until a suitable alternative could be found for Simon.

On 4th January 2014, we again visited the Rehab, but without Joel's father. He had been drinking, which was a disappointment. We had located Adam's step-father and arranged to pick him up, but on the visitation day, he wasn't at the meeting point. I refused to go without him as images of Adam's distress during our previous visit, came back to me. Two of us went to his house leaving everyone else waiting in the van. It was a wooden shack house in the middle of an open area and there was nobody at home. However, as we turned around, I saw the man I recognised from pictures the family had taken as Adam's step-father. He was with two younger children. We reminded him of the visit, but he said he couldn't come as he had to guard a neighbour's property. I looked to where he pointed, which was basically an old pile of bricks which didn't require a guard! Then I saw another neighbour and asked whether he couldn't guard it instead, but the man restated that he wasn't going to come and I realised it was just an excuse.

I got quite animated and told him how upset Adam had been last time, and that he was the only person that might want to visit him. At this point, he told us that he wasn't a relation at all. Adam's relations were in another area and didn't want anything to do with him. I was really fed up of hearing these excuses from one parent after another. I ended up practically begging the man to come with us, but he refused. We suggested one of the children could come instead, as they were Adam's half-siblings. Therefore, although less than satisfactory, this idea seemed better than nothing, so the boy (aged about 10) came with us to see Adam. The man, whom we believed was Adam's step-father, told us that he didn't want Adam returning to live with him, as he was afraid of him and what he might do. Adam had told us previously that he was badly beaten by his step-father which is one of the reasons he had run away in the first place.

When we arrived at the Rehab, Adam was pleased to see his sibling, but unfortunately somebody told him what had happened with his step-father and how I had tried to persuade him to come. I had wanted to keep that a secret from him, in case it would hurt him because of his extreme emotion during the previous visit, but he showed no visible reaction to this information in any event.

The boys were beginning to struggle in the Rehab and starting to misbehave. Paul struggled with depression due to boredom and the others were desperate to get out. They said it had been especially hard over Christmas, as they had had no visitors which reminded them of their loneliness. They also mentioned how our previous visit had been short, due to traffic delays, and that this had made things more difficult. This was a hard visit, as the boys were subdued, but we tried to make the best of it.

At this time, I again thought about my idea to get local churches involved with visiting the children at the Rehab. I had a look at a map to see which churches were nearby. The name of one of the nearest churches rang a bell in my mind, and I realised that it was the new church of the Pastor from Olongapo that had helped us on the bridge with the boys before. I knew him quite well and knew he definitely had a heart for this type of ministry. I sent him a long email all about the Rehab and the ministry, and I asked if the church would consider a regular visiting schedule at the centre, as the staff members were very keen on the idea. He responded after a few days, saying he was excited by the possibility and that maybe some of the church team could accompany us to meet the staff at the Rehab. I was elated and looked forward to this meeting and tying things up.

At around this time, for a number of reasons, the Christian family decided that they could no longer have the boys living back at their house after Rehab. The family wanted to focus on their own ministry as a family and for their older boys to go to work. They were concerned that there would be no-one at the house to supervise the boys when they were all working and that this might lead to problems. I agreed with this observation, but I was worried about how to tell the boys and explain what had been decided. I was also worried about taking over the co-ordination and organisation of the monthly visits to the Rehab without the support of the family. Money wasn't an issue but rounding up relatives, preparing food, buying medicine and many other smaller details on my own would be a huge task especially with my limited language ability. The family helpfully agreed to be involved with the preparations as usual, for the visit in February, for which I was grateful as it allowed me some time to make decisions about the longer term future of the ministry.

During our visit in February 2014, I knew I had to inform Paul, Joel, and Adam that they would not be able to return to the family in Olongapo. This was especially tough as it was so close to them being released, only a few months to go. When we got there, we found that Paul and Simon were on restriction. Paul was on restriction, for being rude to one of the guards, and Simon for fighting. Paul said that he had been rude because he was bored and didn't want to exercise that day. I told him he must behave himself or they might keep him in there for more time, which none of us wanted. Adam, who was usually in trouble for fighting, was doing well with good reports.

I spoke to Paul first and explained the whole situation about the family. He took it well, but I think it was because he knew that I would still be there for him. He requested that I try and find him a Christian foster family because he was worried about returning to the Centre for Youth due to the influences and pressures of former friends. I said that I would do my best but I couldn't promise anything as this was a tough thing to ask. Joel was next and promptly burst into tears. He was just so disappointed, having pinned all of his hopes on going back to the family. However, I knew this would pass as he had only spent two days at their house before. Deep down, I was hoping that he would return home in due course, maybe with financial support. Adam said that he didn't mind and that he was happy to go back to the Centre for Youth.

I then spoke to Joel's father alone with the social worker. I mentioned our previous visit and how we had received reports that he hadn't attended due to being drunk. We were looking for him to take responsibility for Joel, but he wasn't taking responsibility even for himself. I said this carefully thinking that he might react against the accusation, but he accepted my observation. He said that he is easily influenced by his friends, but I told him that was unacceptable due to his age, and the fact he has a young wife and three small children in addition to Joel. We spoke about mistreatment in the past and how Joel was afraid of him. He admitted having been careless with him in the past. I then shared my personal testimony with him, as it felt like the right thing to do. I shared how I had also been hopeless and lost in a world of drink and other vices, and how Jesus had changed my life. The social worker asked him how he felt about my story, and he said he was overwhelmed by it. I could see he was really listening. I invited him to bring his family to the church the following day.

I didn't know if I would see the family members again, so in the van on the way back, I invited all of the relatives to church and gave them Bibles. I wasn't sure if we would organise another visit with the van now that the Christian family were not involved, due to the cost, organisational requirements and the fact that the first batch of boys would be leaving the Rehab very soon.

36: "Rugby Boys" in Church

The following morning, when I arrived at the church, the Pastor said that someone had been there already asking if this was "Natalie's church," and that he had gone back to get his whole family. After a few minutes, Joel's dad, step-mum, and the three small children walked into the church. It was such a moving moment when they all traipsed in. They have been back to the church since that date and Simon's dad and sister have also attended. I pray that they will really understand the Gospel and not just attend the church, but it is a great first few steps.

I invited the older boys that I knew from the street to come to the church with me. Several of them said that they would, but didn't turn up. I knew that I would have to accompany them to get them to attend. During a heart to heart with James, the boy who kept getting a job and then losing it in an earlier chapter, I said that if he really wanted to change his life once and for all he should come to church with me that Sunday. To my surprise, he agreed and told me to collect him outside MCD's at 9am on Sunday. I remembered this appointment just in time, and turned up to find nobody there. I asked his brother, who was working nearby, and he told me James was asleep in a Jeepney and he would take me there.

When I arrived, I saw that there were some boys asleep in the back of the Jeepney stretched out over the seats, with a lot of adult men hanging around chatting. There were three boys: James, Caleb (12), and a boy I didn't know called Esau. I had met Caleb only a few weeks prior for the first time. I had heard about him already because he had been released from Rehab and, within a few weeks, was back on the street abusing solvents. I knew that there was now another Court Order to send him back. It was all such a waste. I tried to convince him he should go and talk to the social workers and apologise, but he kept saying "tomorrow", and I knew he would end up back in Rehab.

I woke the boys up and told them we were going to church in a voice that said, "Don't argue with me." This resulted in shocked looks on the faces of the adult males, as a white foreign female had just instructed a load of street boys that they were going to church. The boys got up and started wiping their faces and looking confused, but they agreed to come. I took them to MCD's first and bought them food. Then we got straight into a Jeepney and went to church. On the way, I accidentally walked into the roof of a house, banging my head, which they thought was highly amusing, especially as I had been concerned about a bruise on Caleb's head. Now I would probably have one too.

They looked a bit out of place in the church, but people welcomed them and asked their names. The church even gave them new T-shirts to replace their dirty holey ones. They were a bit subdued at first, probably wondering what they were doing there, as it had all happened while they were still half asleep. They came to life when the Pastor asked people if they had anything they wanted to thank God for. The boys then started poking me and telling me to stand up and share my blessing, which I refused to do. Shortly after that, and during the sermon which was in English, they all fell asleep. Later, I gave James his own personal New Testament which he was pleased about.

On leaving church, James asked me to visit one of his friends in the police cells with him. I agreed, and the four of us went to the police station in the city centre. On getting permission to go in and talk to the prisoners, we found that there were eight men in one cell about three metres square. James was proudly carrying his new Bible, but the prisoners caught sight of it and they all wanted one too. I promised to return another day, but they said they were being transferred out to the prison the following day. Then I agreed to go back and get the Bibles and bring them back in a few hours. The guards agreed to this, but only if they also could have copies. Therefore, I ended up giving everyone in the station New Testaments, including a lady who was making a complaint in the station because when she saw me giving them out, she also asked for one.

James stayed with me as we went to the Centre for Youth with some youth from the church. We had planned a social activity for the church youth to meet the street youth. The guys at the centre, especially Solomon and Isaac, were excited to see James, whom they knew from the street as one of their leaders. He stayed and played games with all of us. However, the church youth were shocked by some of the language used by the street youth and during a friendly game of basketball one of the street youth challenged one of the church youth to a fight over a misdirected throw!

James later asked me if I would like to visit his family home. I said, "Yes, of course." and asked some church members to accompany us. On arriving at his house, it turned out it was his sister's birthday. On seeing James, she obviously faced a variety of mixed emotions as she screamed with delight as she hugged him, then punched him in anger, and then burst into tears. James' family lived in a really nice house although there were many people living there and it was at the top of a very dark concrete staircase with over one hundred steps. James' father was already deceased but his mother held a position of influence at work that would easily allow her to find James a good job. But James and his brothers had all rejected this help as they wanted to make it on their own, so to speak, and I had to respect them for this.

James agreed to stay at the house with his family, but he also said he would come back to the church the following Sunday. Although I hoped he would come, he failed to do so. I had learned the three P's to avoid discouragement by now: Patience, Persistence and Prayer. Eight weeks after this, I spoke to James' brother, who confirmed that James was still solvent free and residing at home. I pray that he will not lapse back into his old ways and that he will read the New Testament that I gave him.

37: My Wake Up Call

In February 2014, after a brief visit to England, I returned to Olongapo with my close friend Penny, who was to stay for two weeks. I was now living in an apartment in New Cabalan (45 minutes Jeepney ride from the bridge), and visiting the original bridge ministry site less often as the remaining boys were no longer there. The smaller groups that were left continued to abuse solvents under various bridges, I think because they are relatively discreet places for this type of activity. I asked the police/DSWD a few times where the "rugby boys" had moved to, but no one seemed to know. I hoped, rather than believed, that this meant that they had all stopped the solvent abuse because I knew there would always be some that continued.

Penny and I were walking across one such bridge, in a different part of the city, one early evening, looking for somewhere to eat. Suddenly, out of the corner of my eye, next to the barrier that leads down under this bridge, I saw a dirty and partially clothed figure rush to a green wheelie bin, pull the lid open, rummage around for a few seconds, and then scurry away again. It all happened so quickly that, although I had seen this boy, I didn't really notice or pay much attention and we carried on walking for a few seconds. It was Penny who said, "Maybe he is one of them?" (She was talking about the "rugby boys" as she knew a lot about the ministry I was involved in.) The thought briefly entered my mind that the timing of this encounter was a little inconvenient. This was partly because I was worried about getting Penny involved with this boy. It's one thing to put myself in these situations, but quite another to force someone else into them. To her credit, Penny seemed just as keen as I was to investigate further and so I quickly pushed the thought away.

It was often at inconvenient times that I saw these boys, but when I thought about my other commitments, my priorities were often quickly re-evaluated. After all, what is more important than starting a conversation that may change, or even save, a person's life? There may not be another opportunity for that person to hear about the hope that can only be found in Jesus. To hear that there is any type of hope is often news for these invisible children, who have long since abandoned the hope that they were clinging onto in life. As Christian's, it is almost always "time" that is required to take that first crucial step in reaching out to that lost person. Buying food is often necessary as a tool to open the door to share with them and to demonstrate God's love in action, but it is not the most important factor. We should help practically if we can, as it says in the Bible in James 2:16,

"If you say to your brother," Go, I wish you well, stay warm and well fed," but do nothing about his physical needs, what good is this?"

I mention this not as a lecture or mini sermon but as a reminder to all of us (myself included.) Sometimes I found it difficult to strike the right balance of help and hope when building new relationships with the street boys and other homeless people. There were times when I really was busy or with others who didn't share my concern for them and I was therefore unable to give them my time or attention. For example; In January 2014, when I was on the way to Clark Airport in Angeles City, and I stopped to talk to a large group of very young "rugby boys" but had to walk away afterwards because it was completely out of my working area and I had no contacts there. In my heart I wanted to move there for a few months to work with these boys on a daily basis, but I knew this was unrealistic, and I had to trust that God was looking after these children. I prayed that a local church would take responsibility for ministering to them in due course.

On another occasion, I was rushing to get somewhere and a lady asked me for money to feed her children. Normally, I make it a practice never to give money, as if the person has an addiction it can make things worse, but on this day I gave her a very small amount of money. Afterwards, I was convicted that I had done this partly to get rid of the poor lady because my mind was on other things and I didn't have time for her. I hadn't even told her the reason I was willing to give. This lady probably thought that I was just a rich foreigner or kind stranger. Either way, it was useless spiritually. I thought about this a lot later and decided that whenever I gave anything in future I would always take the time to share the reason for my help even if it was hope in very basic terms, for example, "Jesus loves you and this is from Him."

There were also times on the ship when I had very little money and was unable to help practically. I had to learn to accept these things and realise that I could not do everything. I recall being upset one day as I had stopped to talk to an older homeless lady. Afterwards, I felt totally useless as I couldn't offer her what she really needed practically. However, I was able to encourage her to seek God for her needs and to attend the local church. A friend reminded me that we should help practically "when we can" and not allow the enemy to discourage us when we can't.

On this day, Penny and I stopped and retraced our steps back to the bridge. I walked around the barrier and down into the dark space underneath it, feeling a tiny bit afraid of what I might find. I moved forward gradually as my eyes adjusted to the darkness and, as I called out, two figures slowly and hesitantly moved towards me. The two boys were really filthy dirty and very thin, aged about 15 or 16. I engaged them in basic conversation, establishing names and that they were living under the bridge.

I could see Penny watching from the bridge. She suggested we get some food, so we took them to a fast food restaurant nearby called "Jollibee" (the Filipino equivalent of McDonald's.) Many local people watched with astonishment as we walked along the street with the boys. They smelt strongly of solvents and seemed a bit dazed and confused. One of the boys had visible traces of glue on his face and in his hair. He was so dirty and dishevelled that he looked almost animal-like, having lost the ability and motivation to care for himself or his appearance. I hadn't seen boys in this state before as my "bridge boys" were relatively clean and lucid in comparison.

We chatted with the boys whilst they ate, which they did slowly. A side effect of the drugs is that they make the children feel full so that when they eat proper food they sometimes feel ill or can't eat much until their bodies re-adjust. It's similar to the effect of not eating at all for a few days. Your stomach shuts down and it's hard to start eating again. I spoke to the boys about the dangers of the solvents and discovered that they knew some of my other boys from the bridge area. We shared the Gospel with them and invited them to attend a local church before leaving.

Although I looked for them, I didn't see these boys again, but I thought about them a lot and kept replaying what had happened in my mind. My only mental comparison was to some kind of animal scurrying around and routing through rubbish. My mind hadn't even registered that they were humans. I could see how easy it was for these boys to become invisible to locals, especially when the sight of them high on drugs and searching through rubbish bins became normal, and blended in with everything else that was happening. I realised with shock that I hadn't really seen these boys. They had become invisible to me, as well as the many other people milling around. I determined and hoped that I would keep my eyes open in the future and not allow this to happen again.

38: Grading Celebration Day

The time arrived for me to visit the Rehab again, as although I had decided not to provide the van anymore, I had made a promise a long time before that I would visit the boys once a month. I planned to visit using public transport, but I felt guilty as I knew that some family members really wanted to see their children, particularly Simon's dad and sister, who had been faithful in their monthly attendance. I knew that they couldn't afford to visit by themselves and that Simon's dad might find it difficult on public transport due to his disability.

In the end, I spoke to the social worker at the Centre for Youth about the situation, she suggested we use one of their vans and drivers to save money. My charity could cover the fuel, food, and anything else required. She also wanted to accompany us, as she hadn't visited the boys at the Rehab for a long time and she was responsible for them. Additionally, the Rehab staff had planned a special celebration for the boys to celebrate the completion of their school year grade, and we were invited.

On 14th March 2014, we attended the celebration at the Rehab in Manila. Simon's father and sister were the only relatives that accompanied us. I was a bit disappointed that Joel's family hadn't made the effort as they had been given advance notice. The Pastor from the local church who wanted to begin ministry in the centre, also joined us on this day, with five ladies from his church. This was a real encouragement as they met some of the boys and the staff at the centre. They hope to begin a formal children's programme at the Rehab in due course.

The Rehab boys looked smart in their white T-shirts and trousers, prepared specially for the occasion. I was pleased that they seemed to be in better spirits than the previous visit and were looking forward to their release. The celebration began just after we arrived, and then continued for hours with many long speeches from various important looking officials. The boys looked pretty bored and kept attempting to join us at the tables nearby where we were waiting to eat the food we had brought for them, but every-time they thought the speeches had finished someone else stood up to speak and they were forced to traipse dejectedly back to their seats.

For the main event, the boys' names were called out one at a time and they walked in single file onto the stage to be presented with their certificates. Adam completed Kindergarten, Simon and Joel, grade two and three, and Paul grade four. Afterwards, there were special awards for leadership and good behaviour. Several of our boys received medals, including Paul, who asked me to stand on stage with him as his petitioner. I was honoured to do this, but some of the other boys in the audience thought it was funny because I'm obviously not his parent, so there was an audible undercurrent of sniggering as we walked together. I felt slightly uncomfortable for Paul's sake, but he didn't seem bothered by this and just ignored them, collected his medal, had his photo taken and that was that.

Later, as we were eating, Joel requested permission for Isaac and Solomon to join us. In the hype and activity, I had forgotten that they had already been transferred to the centre from Olongapo just a week earlier. I immediately asked the social worker if they could join us, because we had brought food for them. After ten minutes the two boys appeared, their heads having been shaved. I was shocked to see them so physically altered from the lively naughty boys that had been rushing around the Centre for Youth trying to escape only a week prior. They looked small, afraid, dazed, and confused, as if the life had been sucked out of them. I nearly cried when I saw them. They cheered up a little when they saw the big group of us waiting for them, and when I gave them a canteen slip with some money deposited.

After we had finished eating, I was sitting next to Isaac, the youngest of our boys at Rehab, who looked really sad, and then he said something to me in Tagalog. The social worker translated it, but then everyone looked sad. He said, "Ma'am Natalie, when I can come back to Olongapo, I want to come and live with you at your house." The social worker told him that he would have to stay at the centre for a year and he burst into tears. I tried to comfort him without crying myself. This was one of the toughest boys when he was on the street, but reality had set in for him straight away. What he was really saying was, "Ma'am Natalie. Please give me another chance to do the right thing and take me away from this place." Unfortunately, I had no control over his detention as there were Court Orders for all of the boys to be there. However, I promised to visit him every month and encouraged him to pray when he felt alone or to talk to the Christian social workers. He continued crying broken-heartedly for a while as he adjusted to the new information about his detention. Then it was time for us to leave so he turned and gave me a big hug.

As we were leaving, a social worker asked for my full name because the Director of the Rehab had asked who I was as he had seen me with the boys and on the stage with Paul. The social worker told him about the work we had been doing and that my charity was responsible for donating the sleeping mats for the boys. The Director wanted to give some formal recognition of the help I had given them. I jokingly advised the social worker that, rather than recognising me, I would prefer it if the Director made sure the boys didn't have scabies on my next visit. Then thinking better of this and wanting to preserve my good relationship with the Rehab staff, I quickly withdrew my comment and gave my full name but requested no formal recognition. I couldn't think of anything worse than being hauled on stage and "recognised," but I knew that this was a big part of Filipino culture and I didn't want to offend anyone unnecessarily!

On this day, my emotions got the better of me as I walked out through the main gate. I had been suppressing them whilst inside in an effort not to upset the boys. It was just so hard to leave the new boys there, knowing that they would go through the same experience as our other boys over the next twelve months. I reminded myself that the others had looked and behaved like that when they were first at the Rehab. But over time they had really matured and developed into responsible young men due to the enforced discipline and strict regimes at the centre.

Conditions at the Rehab may not be great but the routines and daily devotions are good for the boys and help to prepare them for life in the real world. They also receive a year of

Education. For some, this is their first year of schooling at the age of 15! Some of the staff are Christian and really care for the children and no doubt pray for them as well. This makes a huge difference for these rejected children, who form strong bonds with the social workers. It's just so hard to see them broken first, especially when they are just 11 or 12. However, both Solomon and Isaac had had many chances in Olongapo, and I realised that this was the only way for them to learn their lesson and to stay off the street, and the solvents.

39: End of an Era

In March 2014, I began to believe that God was moving me on from Olongapo, to another area of work in Manila. I started to finalise the ministry in Olongapo and made small attempts to help the families of the Rehab boys prepare for the return of their children. I used charity funds to replace the roof on Simon's family's shack house, because it had been severely damaged in a flood, and paid one month rent arrears for Joel's family.

It was then that I received a long awaited message from the Centre for Youth staff. Reuben had finally been located! I had spent many hours searching for him in the highways and byways since returning to Olongapo. I couldn't forget the ingrained memory of him alone, sad, and miserable when I left on the last occasion, and then the subsequent photos of his lifeless expression sent to me by the family. My searches were fruitless, and I thought that maybe he had gone to live elsewhere. Then I heard rumours of local sightings and started to hope that he might be found before I left.

Apart from having to go to the hospital for some tests, and feeling a bit under the weather, the staff said that he was okay and wanted to see me. As in the case of Joel, old hostilities were soon forgotten after even a small lapse of time. I visited him straight away and got half a hug as the other boys were there and he had to consider his image! Then I gave him a photo of us from the bridge days and I saw the appreciative smile before he managed to hide it as it's not "cool" to be excited about things like that. He ate three of the apples and two of the oranges that I brought in quick succession, and then began demanding that I buy him a music speaker! Things hadn't changed at all! I declined, not feeling the need to give him a reason but knowing that he would have no use for it in Rehab as it would be confiscated. I was glad I wouldn't be there when they told him his next destination, but I planned to visit him when he got there!

I visited the Rehab alone in April, a big task as nine Olongapo boys appeared to see me and I had to try and communicate with them all with my still very basic Tagalog. This visit was especially difficult as the boys were hoping to leave, but I had no positive news for them as papers were still being processed. They were also hoping to see family members but of course now that I was moving to Manila the van run would need to be organised by someone else. I offered to continue funding the trip if DSWD wanted to co-ordinate it. The social worker was keen to continue this but their vehicle had broken down with no definite date for repair so the plan was postponed.

After this visit charity funds paid for Paul to have a series of medical tests with a view to a potential transfer to a Christian Children's Home in Manila. He had expressed concern about returning to Olongapo and potentially succumbing to influences and vices from his past and I wanted to give him another option. I also received paperwork in relation to the transfer suggesting that Paul was two years older than I had originally believed. On the street, this wouldn't have been big news as the boys often lied about their ages but Paul had consistently told us that he was 14 when we first met him, which meant that he was about to turn 16. However, this new information, (if true), made him about to turn 18 instead! On discussion, it was clear that he didn't know this and definitely believed that he was 15 turning 16. At my request, the social worker launched an investigation to determine the truth.

The transfer didn't go ahead in the end for a number of reasons. The main one was that I felt Paul was going along with the decision to transfer on my advice rather than because he really wanted to. I was concerned about this as I didn't want to be responsible for making his life any more difficult than it already was. I was also worried that he wasn't ready to cut his ties with Olongapo at this stage. He looked so sad at the prospect of being transferred alone and missing his friends that I decided it might not be wise.

We were all expecting Paul's medical test results to be negative, as although he had been diagnosed with TB, this had been over a year before and he had not experienced medical issues at the Rehab. Sadly and surprisingly, he was diagnosed with Hepatitis B for which there is no permanent cure. At around the same time, his release order came through from the court (the first one as the other boys had a different Judge). Throughout this period, I dreaded receiving the result of our enquiry about Paul's age. I knew that potentially I would then have to inform him that in addition to having an incurable disease he had also lost two years of his life!

I visited the boys again towards the end of May 2014. I left the visit until later in the month hoping that I could join the social worker from Olongapo and that some of the boys would be able to be released. However, the service vehicle was still broken in Olongapo so I visited alone again. On arrival the boys were subdued and didn't seem interested in the Jollibee takeaway I had brought them, although they perked up after a while. Simon was upset because his medical release order still hadn't come through from the Judge. I was astounded to hear this because the release had originally been requested in November 2013, on the basis that the Rehab didn't have sufficient resources to care for Simon adequately. It had now been nearly eight months, which was the normal length of time for a child to stay in Rehab!

Then, I discovered that Paul and another Olongapo boy had had a fight earlier in the day. The other boy hit Paul on the head with a rock and Paul punched him in retaliation. Both boys were placed under "violation" and were not allowed to attend the visitation. I was advised that they were both crying in the dormitory.

Unfortunately, Isaac had a severe case of scabies (the worst I had seen) which was especially bad on his hands and feet which were covered in sores and bleeding so he could barely walk. I took him straight to the Rehab clinic and paid for additional medicine but there was little else I could do and he seemed cheerful enough.

Other than this, the visit was pretty relaxed as the boys that were due for release knew that it would happen eventually and the new boys had settled down and were looking forward to starting school in June. Joel stated his earnest desire never to go back to the street or solvents and told me he was praying for me. The boys quoted Bible verses they had learnt in devotions and repeated the lyrics of Christian songs. I left them some Gospel Tracts that I had with me and they immediately started reading them aloud. I was so encouraged by the discussions this day and by their obvious enthusiasm for Christian things. One older boy even told me that he had become a Christian in the Rehab through a Chaplain or staff member.

I had been preparing for the release of the first group of boys for a long time, having seen the journey begin. They were definitely ready to leave, and I was ready to help them get on with their lives in the real world. Looking back, it seemed like a lifetime ago when I first went to that place and saw those small, confused, fearful faces and had to hold back the tears. The difference in the boys now - both physically due to the absence of drugs- and in character due to the discipline was stark. I dared to hope that they had also been changed spiritually but ultimately this is the work of God and I had to leave this in His hands.

On this day in May, I once again walked out through the metal gated partition separating the Rehab boys from the rest of the world. Then I headed up the hill towards the entrance gate. I turned and waved several times whilst walking up the hill and the boys reciprocated as they walked down the hill in the opposite direction back to their dormitory. I noticed a few boys looking back several times to see if I was still there, seeking their individual goodbyes. If they were feeling especially lonely or sad they would keep looking back until I had completely disappeared through the entrance gate. These were the times that I found it hard to leave them there. However, on this day, I was reminded that God would take care of them because, "In His hand is the life of every creature and the breath of all mankind." Job 12 vs 10.

Epilogue

When I arrived in Subic Bay in March 2012, I had no idea what was in store for me. If someone had told me in advance that I was to spend the next two years and beyond expending my best energies and emotions on the plight of a few street teenage boys, I would have laughed. If that same person had told me of the emotional ups and downs and frustrations I would have to go through in order to see just a little bit of change in just a few lives, maybe I would have reconsidered getting involved. But looking back, I can say that it has honestly been worth it. A few lives have changed drastically, and in others there have been small gradual changes over time. But each of these boys is precious to God and He desires that, "none of them should be lost but that each of them should come to repentance." 2 Peter 3 vs 9.

I have learnt many lessons along the way, and after only two years working with these boys, I am no expert. I have made many mistakes, most of which are documented here, and a few of which are not! I hope that after reading this book you might be able to think of ways to make a difference in the life of one or more of these "invisible" children. My biggest piece of advice is "start small," One of the smallest things we did which had the biggest impact was to learn the names of the boys and to use them. Whoever God calls you to help, I encourage you to treat them as individuals and demonstrate through this that their lives are important. Constantly remind them that it is God who loves them and that this is the reason for your concern. Don't expect dramatic change straight away, but; be Patient, Persevere, and Pray. Don't try and do everything, or you will end up doing nothing. Just do something. One person put it like this:

"I am only one, but still I am one. I cannot do everything, but still I can do something; and because I cannot do everything, I will not refuse to do something that I can do."   Helen Keller

In April 2014, I left Olongapo and moved to Cubao in Manila to begin working with Cubao Reformed Baptist Church amongst the street homeless people and the "rugby boys." The motto of Christian Compassion Ministries, the charity of my new church is "How can we tell people about the love of Christ without showing them something of that love?" This resonated within me and tied in perfectly with my charity's slogan "Help and Hope must go hand in hand."

I knew that I would visit Olongapo from time to time because part of my heart remained there with the boys, at home with their families, at the Centre for Youth and with those still on the street. I had committed to being there for these boys if ever they needed help. I was determined to keep that promise, especially to those boys who had no one else, and to be a reliable and consistent figure in their lives as a constant reminder of God's love and care for them through His people.

In my experience, at the end of a true story like this, the reader is often left wondering what has happened to the people mentioned within. How did their lives turn out? Of course, only God knows their long-term future but you can keep abreast of developments here:

www.facebook.com/groups/olongapochristianhelpandhope

The Individual Boys

The Individuals

(In the order they first appear and at the age we believed them to be when we first met them)

Matthew (18)

Matthew was the main group leader that we spent a lot of time with as he appeared at the start of our ministry on the bridge. He has been on and off the street for many years. He has been to Rehab at least twice and claims he became a Christian through a social worker during one of his Rehab stints. He has massive problems with his family and can't live with them.

Matthew is still working in Olongapo City at various low paying jobs. Many of the older boys sell counterfeit DVD's in the city for just 100 pesos (£1.40) a day and Matthew is often amongst them. However, he is believed to be solvent free at this time.

Noah (9)

Noah was the youngest of our boys and the only one of our regulars attending school and not abusing solvents. He was in danger of becoming one of the next generation of "rugby boys" due to the amount of time he spent with them, but during our time on the bridge he didn't succumb. His mother was working near to the bridge, hence the connection.

Noah is still living with his mother in the general vicinity of the bridge and is still attending school. He no longer hangs around with the group of boys as the group was disbanded during our work with the bridge boys. The last time I saw him, he was with his older brother and wearing his school uniform.

Rachel (16) and Jacob (17)

Rachel and Jacob appeared to be in a relationship. Initially, Jacob was always hanging around, sniffing solvents, begging, and making a nuisance of himself, but eventually he found a job and left the street. Rachel only appeared a few times on the bridge and was already holding a steady job.

I did not see Rachel or Jacob during my return visits to Olongapo City. I pray that they are still working and that Jacob has not returned to his former ways.

David (21)

David was another of the main group leaders and was good friends with Matthew. They had spent time in Rehab together. David left the street early in our ministry, responding to his realisation that God loved him. He made a profession of faith and began attending a local Baptist Church. He found a stable job and stayed well away from his former vices for over a year.

In 2014, David's friends reported that he was using solvents and drinking, and that he was no longer attending the church. David advised me that he planned to attend the church on Easter Sunday and states that he is not back to his former ways. He is still working full time.

James (20)

James was another of our main group leaders but was less attached to the group. James appeared at the bridge at times but then left again. He was also abusing solvents. James obtained various low paid jobs during our time with him, including selling food that he had cooked, but these were always short lived and he didn't seem able to hold a job for longer than a few weeks at a time.

James came to a Church in Olongapo in 2014 and I was invited to his house and met his family. His dad had died a while ago. He seemed serious about changing his life, and his friends report that he has stayed at home and is not inhaling solvents.

Mark (16)

Mark was one of our biggest struggles. He claimed to be "born again" and had been attending Church and Bible study but, after an incident involving a girl in July 2012, he dropped out of high school in his final year, began inhaling solvents, and living on the street. We began our ministry at around this time, not knowing that Mark was a newcomer. Mark has a mother, father, and brother, and his own room at the family home (unusual amongst this group of boys.) His father works abroad and his mother also works selling food in the city.

Mark went home in 2013 and remains there with his family. He re-enrolled at school and completed his final year. He plans to attend college. He is solvent free. He states he is attending Church again.

Joel (12)

Joel was the leader of the younger group and had a lot of influence over the others. He was also using solvents daily. He had a good brain and used it to maintain control and to manipulate people. He had a family (dad, step-mother, and 3 half siblings) living about thirty minutes away from the bridge area. He was upset about the break-up of his parent's marriage, which is the original reason he ran away to the street.

Joel is preparing to leave Rehab, having spent over a year there. He has made a profession of faith. He will return to the Centre for Youth in Olongapo and attempts will be made to continue rebuilding his relationship with his father from the centre. He wants to continue his studies started in the Rehab and will attend school from the youth centre in June 2014.

Adam (15?)

Adam became one of our regular boys, although we didn't see him much at first. He had some kind of learning difficulty and always seemed to be alone. He was upset that his family had sent him to live with his uncle and "just thrown him away like a piece of rubbish." His "uncle" gave him money daily for food and sometimes he disappeared for a few days, probably returning to his "uncle's" house. We couldn't locate the "Uncle." We were unsure of his age and he didn't know it either. He was also abusing solvents.

Adam is preparing to leave Rehab after over a year spent in residence there. He had requested to stay there for another year, having developed a strong bond with one of the Christian social workers, but later changed his mind when she felt that she needed to tell him that she couldn't be with him 24/7. Adam really just wants his own family. He will go back to the Centre for Youth in Olongapo and continue his studies, as he has just completed Kindergarten at the Rehab.

Simon (12)

Simon was one of our regular boys and was definitely the one with the cheekiest grin. He was well liked in the group and had had a better up-bringing than some of the others. His parents were separated and his Dad disabled (suffering from polio), resulting in the family struggling to put food on the table. Simon had been collecting plastic to sell but got involved with the "rugby boys" due to peer pressure and failed to return home. Simon was abusing solvents every day.

In 2013, Simon was diagnosed with an enlarged heart due to solvent abuse. He will soon secure a medical release from Rehab and will return to live with his father and sister. Olongapo Christian Help and Hope has financed his ongoing medical costs to date and, in addition, has recently financed a new roof for the family house. Simon will attend school on his return to Olongapo. He also has made a profession of faith.

Solomon (11)

Solomon was with us every day to start with, and we helped him with a medical incident. Shortly after this, in August 2012, he left the bridge and went back to school for a while. He was from a poorer area outside the city and he had 8 siblings. The family didn't have enough food. He was abusing solvents daily.

In late 2013, Solomon re-appeared on the street and was sent to Rehab in March 2014. He will spend a year in Rehab.

Reuben (11)

Reuben was different to some of the other boys because he was a lot younger in himself and really just wanted to play games all of the time. He had been on and off the street since he was just 7. His family lived a long way from the area and he suffered from physical violence at home. He had a stubborn streak though, which was hard to combat at times, but he was also very likeable.

Reuben almost settled with our Christian family, but became restless and ran away. He also escaped from the Centre for Youth a number of times and returned to locate his family, only to find they had moved away and he doesn't know where they have gone. He is back at the Centre for Youth now and will be transferred to Rehab within the next month or so. He will be released next year (2015.)

Joshua (10)

Joshua was the youngest boy abusing solvents. He was Muslim, but we only discovered this after working with the boys for some time. He had family locally and sometimes disappeared for a week when his father caught him and took him home, but he was harshly punished and escaped again as soon as he could.

I was informed that Joshua's family had moved to Manila, having been made homeless in Olongapo, but in March 2014 I was told that Joshua had been seen with his mother at the local market. There are no reports to suggest he is still using solvents.

Luke (15)

Luke was one of the saddest cases because he had a genuine reason for being on the street. He was from a Muslim family and his father had died the previous year. He had only been on the street since his father died, but hadn't been to school for many years. His family was extremely poor and lived in cramped conditions with many relatives. He was a likeable boy and he often looked after the younger boys, but he was also easily influenced in a negative way and was addicted to the solvents.

Luke moved to Manila with his mother in 2013 to attend an Islamic school. My last contact with him in 2013 was online when he said he was unhappy and wanted to come back to Olongapo. He also told me that he wasn't in school, but I haven't heard anything from him since. I pray that he is doing well now.

Malachi (9)

Malachi wasn't using solvents when I first met him in 2012, and he only appeared a few times at the bridge. He was often misrepresenting his physical condition in order to beg from local people.

Malachi began using solvents in 2013 and was taken to the Centre for Youth. He will be transferred to Rehab soon, having run away from the Centre back to the street several times. He will be the youngest boy from Olongapo at the Rehab.

Isaac (11)

Isaac was one of the toughest of the younger boys and didn't like to show his affection for us. He only appeared at the bridge a few times in our ministry. He has wealthy family connections, but his parents are separated and there are problems at his current home. He was often in a different part of town abusing solvents alone.

Isaac was taken to the Centre for Youth and later transferred to Rehab with Solomon in March 2014. The initial shock immediately broke his hard exterior. He will be released next year (2015.)

Paul (14)

Paul was probably the boy that changed the most during our time working with the group. Paul was aggressive, obnoxious, and difficult to handle at first. He just used us for what he could get and constantly tested our boundaries. He had been on and off the street since he was 7. His mother left when he was a baby and his father took solvents, developed mental health problems, and later went to prison. Paul was left in the care of an older couple in the neighbourhood, but the male later died. Paul ran away from one Christian Orphanage due to bullying. He was addicted to solvents and had spent a year in Rehab at the age of 11. He was diagnosed with TB at the hospital with us in 2012. Over-time, Paul changed his attitude towards us and became very loyal. He decided to leave the street and made a profession of faith. He lived with our Christian family for several months, but made a foolish decision to run away and was caught and sent to Rehab in Manila.

Paul has been in Rehab since Feb 2013 and is about to leave. Unfortunately he was recently diagnosed with Hepatitis B and there is a question mark over his age. Paul will return to Olongapo to continue his education and will live at the Centre for Youth.

About the Author

Natalie was raised in a Christian home in West Sussex, England to parents, Keith and Kim Vellacott. She had two younger siblings, James and Lauren. She professed faith in Christianity at a young age but fell away from God at 17, having just been baptised. Natalie subsequently spent many years living a worldly lifestyle before being definitely converted at the age of 23.

Career wise, Natalie joined Sussex Police as an officer when she was just 19. Within the police she worked in many departments including Uniform response and patrol, CID (as a detective,) Child Protection and Internal Investigations. After her conversion to Christianity in 2005, Natalie continued to work for Sussex Police and was promoted to Sergeant in 2009.

Natalie found it increasingly difficult to be a Christian in a secular work environment and her focus was gradually changed to mission work. She took part in street evangelism in her spare time and spent many hours sharing her faith with colleagues at work. In 2011, Natalie felt that God was calling her to apply for a two year commitment on the Logos Hope Christian Missionary Ship. She applied for a two year career break from Sussex Police, which was granted, and was subsequently accepted for the Mission, after initially being told she might have to go to Afghanistan instead!

Natalie fulfilled her two year commitment on the Logos Hope (the subject of this book) and as a result of her experiences, subsequently moved to live and work in the Philippines as a full time independent Missionary Evangelist in December 2013. Natalie is currently serving with Cubao Reformed Baptist Church in Metro Manila, working with the street homeless people and teenagers that abuse solvents.

Natalie is the founder and a trustee of the Christian charity "Olongapo Christian Help and Hope" which operates in the UK providing funding for street teenagers in Olongapo and the surrounding areas. Natalie maintains her connections with the "Olongapo boys" and continues to financially support various related projects with charity funds. This book is "not for profit" with all monies being used for the direct support of the Olongapo street teenagers and others needing practical help in the Philippines.

Natalie often uses her personal story as a living testimony of the hope that can be found only in Jesus, inspiring others to seek Him as their source of hope. She seeks to help people find assurance in God's promise of eternal life through the verse in Romans 10 vs 9 "If you confess with your mouth Jesus is Lord and believe in your heart God raised Him from the dead, you WILL be saved."

Natalie's Personal Story

"I became a Christian at a young age primarily due to having been raised in a Christian home and being surrounded by Christianity. As a teenager there were times when I was really serious about my faith. But there were also times when I became distracted from God and I wasn't really building a personal relationship with Him. During a more serious faith phase at the age of 17 I was baptised by full immersion, but just six weeks later fell away from God in a dramatic fashion.

I subsequently spent six years immersed in the "party lifestyle", succumbing to many activities and bad habits that sought to replace God, including an abundance of alcohol, cigarettes, gambling, and the regular watching of violent/horror movies. I moved from one non-Christian relationship to another in an attempt to find happiness which eluded me. I became more and more miserable attempting to ignore God, but knowing deep down that He was really there and that I was under His judgement because of my lifestyle choices.

I began a course in Law and Criminology at Sheffield University in 2000, but dropped out after just six weeks to join Sussex Police, thereby fulfilling a childhood dream. In 2002, my younger brother James (who was a Christian) was tragically killed in a car accident at the age of just 18. My parents clung to their Christian faith at this time, but I became angry with God for allowing this to happen and resented others for judging my lifestyle.

In April 2005, after many other problems and a long struggle, I faced up to the fact that I was miserable and that my life was a total mess. I had recently witnessed my younger sister Lauren going through a mini-version of the same struggles and had seen the resulting contentment when God graciously called her back to Himself and Lauren repented and trusted in Him. I knew that I was carrying the heavy weight of my many sins around on my shoulders every day. I sometimes woke up at night in a terrified state, believing I was going to hell because of the things I had done. I knew that God was waiting for me to repent of my sin and turn back to Him and that He had been patiently waiting for a long time. I lived in constant fear that time would run out and that I may have tested God's grace one too many times. Eventually, God brought me to the end of my resources. All I could do was cry out for His help. I said sorry to God for my many sins. I believed His promise that, 'All who call on the name of the Lord will be saved'. God, by His grace, planted true faith in my heart and I determined to live a new life before Him.

I abandoned my sinful vices immediately and began regularly attending my former church; Worthing Tabernacle. Two Bible verses became very important to me as a result of my experiences. The first is found in John 6 vs 67-68 "You do not want to leave too, do you?" Jesus asked the Twelve. Simon Peter answered him, "Lord, to whom shall we go? You have the words of eternal life." (NIV) These verses remind me that seeking anyone other than Jesus is a total waste of time because He is the only one with the words of eternal life that can offer hope for the future. The second verse is from Mark 8 vs 36 "For what shall it profit a man, if he shall gain the whole world, and lose his own soul?" (KJV) This sums up my life experience as I tried seeking happiness in the world but foolishly risked losing my soul in the process.

When I tell people my story I am often asked "How do you know it was God that brought you back to your faith and not just a decision you made and carried out through your own will and determination?" This is a good question. The truth is that I didn't have the strength or desire to give up my vices, I tried many times to turn my life around and always failed. Although I saw the emptiness and meaninglessness of life without God and the utter futility of daily life lived without purpose, I was powerless to make the big changes I knew were necessary. I was so immersed in my sinful lifestyle that a new start seemed like an impossibility. Before God could help me I had to accept that I needed His help, that I was totally dependent and reliant on Him to restore me and that I couldn't change anything myself. True salvation occurs only when God changes a person's heart allowing them to believe in Him. The Bible says in Matthew 19 vs 26 "With man this is impossible, but with God all things are possible."

God already had His hand on my life, due to my Christian upbringing, former beliefs and the fact that many people were praying for me regularly. God protected me from serious harm throughout this period and from serious long term consequences. Looking back, I am so grateful to God for the mercy, grace and patience that He demonstrated towards me during my rebellion. The Bible says in Ephesians 2 vs 8-9 "By grace you have been saved, through faith and that not of yourselves; it is the gift of God; not of works, lest any man should boast." This is my personal experience and all of the glory for the change in my life goes to God as I wasn't capable of turning my own life around.

I wouldn't be a true evangelist without explaining what it means to become a Christian and how you too can be free of your sin and reconciled to God to spend eternity in heaven with Him one day. During my last few years of Missionary service I was taught a tool to explain the Gospel. It has been effectively used by millions of people around the world. It is called the "Wordless Book" and consists simply of five coloured sheets of paper or material each representing part of the message of salvation found in the Bible.

Yellow: This represents heaven. Do you want everlasting life in Heaven?

The Bible tells us that the streets in heaven are paved with gold. It also tells us that God is light and that in Him there is no darkness and that Jesus (God's only Son) is the light of the world. Heaven is God's dwelling place and the Bible also tells us that no man has ever imagined the wonderful things that God has prepared in heaven for those that love Him.

Heaven is forever.

Black: This represents sin. What is wrong with the world? More importantly, what is wrong with me?

Being honest, we need to face the bad news in order to see the value of the good news. The Bible says that all people have sinned and fall short of the glory of God and that the wages of sin is death.

God is holy and cannot have anything to do with sin. God is righteous and just and therefore cannot just overlook our sin and forgive us because this would make Him unjust. Our sin separates us from God permanently. All sinners are destined to spend an eternity in hell without God. Hell is a truly terrible place where people will long to die because of their torment but will be unable to do so. Hell is forever.

This is the bad news.

Red: This represents the blood of Jesus. Why did Jesus need to die?

God loved us so much that He provided a way of for us to be reconciled to Him and to escape the torments of hell. He sent Jesus His only son to live a perfect life here on earth. It was necessary for a penalty to be paid for our sin. Jesus' purpose in coming was to allow Himself to be sacrificed and punished on a cross in the place of all who believe that He died for them, and who put their trust in Him.

He died instead of them so that they could be free from the guilty sentence hanging over them because of their sin. He died on that cross and then rose from the grave just three days later proving that He had defeated sin and death once and for all. Jesus' death acted as a bridge between guilty sinners and God allowing all who trust in Him to be forgiven for their sins and to live in heaven forever with God.

White: This represents being washed clean from sin. How can be we sure of God's acceptance?

Think of your life as a white sheet. Every-time you sin, even in a small way, a black stain is left on the sheet. When a person becomes a Christian and turns away from their sin, God promises them a new start. He says that he will remember their sins no more.

When God looks at the life of a Christian he sees only Jesus and His righteousness instead of the sin.

Green: This represents growth. How should this change my life?

All true Christians will grow spiritually over time. In order to grow, Christians should regularly read the word of God (the Bible,) pray, attend a church, spend time with other Christians and tell other people about Jesus and His sacrifice for them.

These things do not save people. There are no "divine scales" weighing good and bad deeds as a determining factor for entry to heaven or hell. No human can ever do enough good things to get to heaven as the standard required is perfection, which is why Jesus had to die.

The things described here are the grateful response of a Christian who has been rescued from a life of sin and death and reconciled to God for a life of hope and an eternal future in heaven.

Please contact me if you would like further information.

Maps: Key areas from the book

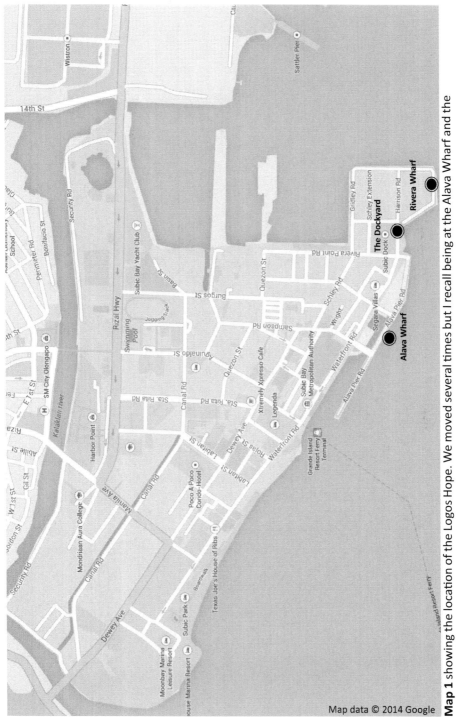

Map data © 2014 Google

Map 1 showing the location of the Logos Hope. We moved several times but I recall being at the Alava Wharf and the Rivera Wharf.

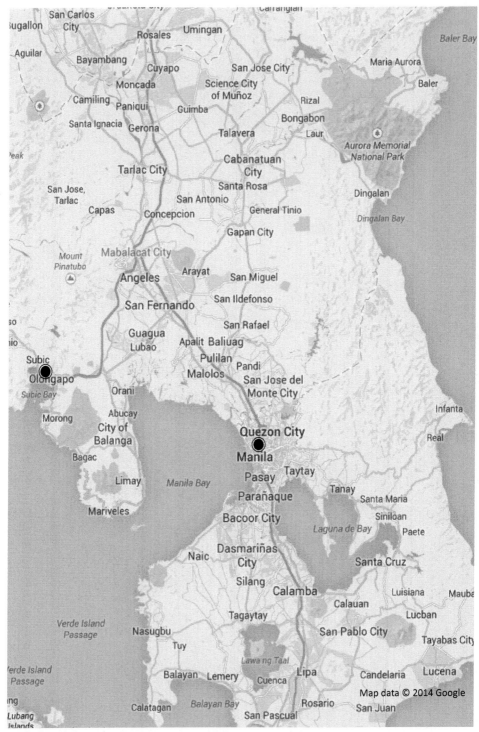

Map 2 showing Olongapo City in relation to Manila. The Rehab centre is located in Manila.

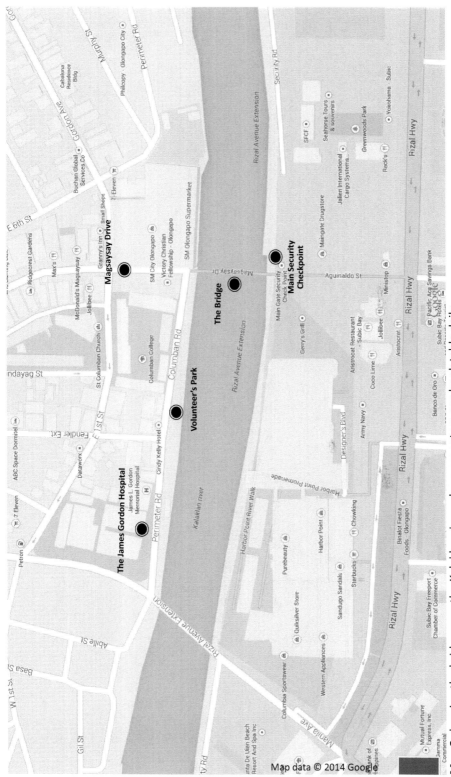

Map 3 showing the bridge over the Kalaklan river where we set up our book table daily.

Map 4 showing a close up of the bridge and surrounding area.

Printed in Great Britain
by Amazon